BOOKS BY EDWARD ABBEY

FICTION
The Fool's Progress
Good News
The Monkey Wrench Gang
Black Sun
Fire on the Mountain
The Brave Cowboy
Jonathan Troy

NONFICTION
Abbey's Road
The Journey Home
Desert Solitaire
Down the River
Beyond the Wall
One Life at a Time, Please
Desert Images (with David Muench)
The Hidden Canyon (with John Blaustein)
Cactus Country (with Ernst Haas)
Slickrock (with Philip Hyde)
Appalachian Wilderness (with Eliot Porter)

An Owl Book

HENRY HOLT AND COMPANY   NEW YORK

BEYOND THE WALL
ESSAYS FROM THE OUTSIDE

EDWARD ABBEY

Henry Holt and Company, LLC
Publishers since 1866
115 West 18th Street
New York, New York 10011

Henry Holt® is a registered trademark
of Henry Holt and Company, LLC.

Library of Congress Cataloging-in-Publication Data
Abbey, Edward, 1927–1989.
Beyond the wall.
ISBN 0-8050-0820-9 (pbk.)
1. West (U.S.)—Description and travel—1951–1980—
Addresses, essays, lectures. 2. West (U.S.)—Description
and travel—1981—Addresses, essays, lectures.
3. Deserts—West (U.S.)—Addresses, essays, lectures.
4. Abbey, Edward 1927–1989—Addresses, essays, lectures.
I. Title.
F595.2A23   1984   917.8'0433   83-18346

Designed by Elissa Ichiyasu

Printed in the United States of America
25 24 23 22 21 20 19 18 17 16 15

Portions of Beyond the Wall have been published
in a somewhat different form and with different
titles in the following magazines and books:
Chapter 1 in GEO, chapter 7 in National Geographic,
and chapter 10 in Outside.
Chapters 2 and 3 in Slickrock (Sierra Club),
chapter 4 in Desert Images (Harcourt Brace
Jovanovich/Chanticleer Press), chapter 6 in
The Hidden Canyon (Viking Penguin, Inc.), and
chapters 8 and 9 in Cactus Country (Time-Life Books).

FOR CLARKE

AND ALL THE OTHER CARTWRIGHTS

CONTENTS

PREFACE

Part of the essay called "A Walk in the Desert Hills" was presented as the fourth annual Belkin Lecture at the University of California, San Diego, in April 1982. An abridged version of this same essay was published in *GEO* in 1983. I wish to thank the trustees of UCSD and the publishers of *GEO* for permission to reprint the entire essay here.

A portion of the essay "Gather at the River" first appeared in *Outside* in the fall of 1983; again I thank the publisher for permission to reprint.

The remaining essays in this book were first published during the 1970s as parts of the text of large-format scenic photography books. (See copyright page for details.) Most of these books were expensive (one retailed for a flat $100); my enemies could buy them but few of my friends. All but *The Hidden Canyon* and *Cactus Country* are now out of print and unavailable. This seemed to me to be adequate justification for recollecting and revising what I feel are the best of the chapters from those books.

Furthermore it is my belief, based on my experience and that of others, that almost nobody bothers to read the words in picture books. Although it may be true, as Confucius said, that one word is worth a thousand pictures (if it's the right word), it is also true that ordinary prose cannot easily share pages with the brilliant work of such camera artists as John Blaustein, Ernst Haas, Philip Hyde and David Muench. Yet my words were written to be seen, ingested, mentally processed. Like any writer I'd rather be read than dead; like all serious authors I'd rather be dead than not read. Therefore I take the liberty of offering these selected essays to the public in a sort of liberated form, free from the domineering, overwhelming presence of true-life, real-color, full-page, scenic-landscape photographs.

The reader will notice that most of these essays deal in one way or another with aspects of the desert. Even the final chapter, an account of a river journey down the North Slope of Alaska, is largely about a region which, because of its low annual precipitation, has been classified by geographers as "Arctic desert." The emphasis on America's arid parts is not an accident.

The problem began sixteen years ago when I published a book of personal narrative called *Desert Solitaire*. That book was written in 1966–67 during a year of wandering from Las Vegas to Hoboken to the Everglades to Death Valley. The final chapters were composed in the corner of a bar serving a legal house of prostitution at Ash Meadows, Nevada, where I waited each day with my little yellow schoolbus (I was the driver) to pick up the children from Shoshone High School for transfer to the village of Furnace Creek in Death Valley. While waiting, I scribbled. A sweet young sexual therapist named Alicia—"whore" seems much too harsh a term—helped me with the big words and other technical matters which the IRS accepted as tax-deductible research. We mailed the thing to New York (book rate), and in January 1968, on a dark night in a back alley in the dead of winter, *Solitaire* was released from its cage and turned loose upon an unsuspecting public.

Nothing happened.

The publisher let the first edition go out of print, and within a year my little book had died a natural death. Not surprised, I found myself a job as a fire lookout on North Rim, Grand Canyon, and continued working for a living.

Three years later, however, *Desert Solitaire* was exhumed and resurrected in paperback, in which form it has enjoyed a modest but persistent life, burrowing along from year to year about two feet underground like a blind and seditious mole. I haven't had to turn my hand to an honest day's work since 1972.

How to explain such queer phenomena? Who knows? I don't much like the book myself; in the author's opinion *Good News*, *Abbey's Road* and *Down the River* are better books—livelier, funnier, more deeply felt, more richly ambiguous, more craftily designed. But as to that, who cares but the author himself? Let the poor scrivening wretch sink ever deeper into his delusions. If you'd care for some really *good* interpretations of the American desert experience I recommend the writings of Colin Fletcher, Ann Zwinger, Barry Lopez, Rob Schulteiss, Ruth Kirk, Edmund Jaeger and Peggy Larson, and the now-classic works of Powell, Dutton, Van Dyke, Austin and Krutch.

No one, so far as I know, has yet attempted to work the American desert into fiction, that is, to make the desert itself—the landscape, the light, the air, the desert's primordial inhabitants—an essential character in a novel. Probably it cannot be done. As for myself, diverted sixteen years ago into desert digressions, I have no intention of writing anything more on so barren and desiccated a subject. This book is my last to be "writ in sand." Never again will I vandalize the slipface of a dune with my impertinent signature. I have nothing new to say about vultures, stone, scorpions, kissing bugs, alkali, silence, death or the sphinxlike Medusa rock that waits for the unwary at the head, the dead end, the ultimate cul-de-sac, of Skeleton Gulch. Let other younger, more hopeful voices carry on.

In any case it is not necessary to read a book to enjoy our strange Western deserts. In fact it is better, I think, to enter the desert the first time with a clean, clear mind devoid of preconceptions, so far as possible. Afterward you may wish to compare your adventures and your response with others, as recorded in books.

Fortunately the American desert remains open to all, most of it still our public domain. No passports needed, no examinations to undergo, no special equipment required, no experience necessary. A journey into the wilderness is the freest, cheapest, most nonprivileged of pleasures. Anyone with two legs and the price of a pair of war surplus combat boots ($17.95) may enter. You will never see a "Public Property—Keep Out" sign in the back of beyond.

First you might prefer to get a broad overview from an airplane or distant passing views from an automobile or a commercial raft trip down a public river. But to get past the superficial, two-dimensional, merely aesthetic experience you must, eventually, leave the mechanical conveyances behind and venture into the rock, cactus and forbidden hills on foot. (A horse will do but is considerable trouble; horses are such delicate, sensitive, spooky creatures.) If you desire to know, feel and live the desert, as opposed to only looking at it as tourists and art critics do, you've got to arise from your bottom end and walk upright like a human being, alone or with a friend, into the ancient blood-thrilling primeval freedom of those vast and democratic vistas. You will never understand the secret essence of the word *freedom* until you do.

This question of muscle and will versus motors and money is still a sore issue with some. Like other natural conservatives I have been accused of "elitism" by those who think that their up-per-bracket incomes give them the special right to drive their Jeeps, Blazers, Broncos and Winnebagos anywhere and every-where. The opposite is the truth: any poor slob with enough cash in his jeans to buy a ghetto blaster can buy instead a backpack, a sleeping bag and a bus ticket to Yellowstone. But only the afflu-ent—the financial elite—can afford the heavy expense of ATCs, ATVs, RVs and ORVs. Machines are domineering, exclusive, de-structive and costly; it is they and their operators who would deny the enjoyment of the back country to the rest of us. About 98 per cent of the land surface of the contiguous USA already belongs to heavy metal and heavy equipment. Let us save the 2 per cent—that saving remnant. Or better yet, expand, recover and reclaim much more of the original American wilderness. About 50 per cent would be a fair and reasonable compromise. We have yielded too much too easily. It is time to start shoving cement and iron in the opposite direction before the entire na-tion, before the whole planet, become one steaming, stinking, overcrowded high-tech ghetto. Open space was the fundamental heritage of America; the freedom of the wilderness may well be the central purpose of our national adventure.

Of course that is only one man's opinion. But shared, I suspect, by about 100 million (or more) of my fellow citizens.

Seventeen years after the writing of *Desert Solitaire* I find no reason to modify my position on the major controversy that was intentionally inflamed, with malice aforethought, by that deliber-ately subversive book. My only regret is that the book was too polite, too meek and mild.

Meanwhile the bad has become worse and the good is still on the defensive. Arches National Monument, for example, has become a travesty called Arches National Park—a static diorama seen through glass. The mining industry has transformed and malformed the fine old farm-and-ranch community of Moab, Utah, into a typical commercial-industrial slum. The nuclear-power-and-weapons Mafia is attempting to establish a radioactive-waste dump in the heart of the Canyonlands. Uranium is being mined right now in the northwest drainages of the Grand Canyon—the only Grand Canyon on earth. For example. And in fact and in short and in sum the entire American West— property of all Americans, home of the wild things, last stronghold of the Ghost Dancers—lies under massive assault by the industrial armies of Government and Greed.

We need no more words on the matter. What we need now are heroes. And heroines. About a million of them. One brave deed is worth a thousand books. Sentiment without action is the ruin of the soul. Or as an old friend of mine once said,

If I regret anything, it is my good behavior.
What demon possessed me that I behaved so well?

So much for all that. Now I can do no more than offer one final prayer to the young, to the bold, to the angry, to the questing, to the lost.

Beyond the wall of the unreal city, beyond the security fences topped with barbed wire and razor wire, beyond the asphalt belting of the superhighways, beyond the cemented banksides of our temporarily stopped and mutilated rivers, beyond the rage of lies that poisons the air, there is another world waiting for you. It is the old true world of the deserts, the mountains, the forests, the islands, the shores, the open plains. Go there. Be there. Walk gently and quietly deep within it. And then—

May your trails be dim, lonesome, stony, narrow, winding and only slightly uphill. May the wind bring rain for the slickrock potholes fourteen miles on the other side of yonder blue ridge. May God's dog serenade your campfire, may the rattlesnake and the screech owl amuse your reverie, may the Great Sun dazzle your eyes by day and the Great Bear watch over you by night.

EDWARD ABBEY
Oracle, Arizona
October 1983

BEYOND THE WALL

ONE

A WALK IN
THE DESERT HILLS

Two friends drive me ten miles into the desert, north from the highway, away from the bus stop where they had met me on my arrival. We had planned to go farther together, thirty miles, to a place called Stone Tanks— the first natural water hole—but the unmarked dirt road becomes obscure, then difficult, soon impossible. If we drive any farther we'll wreck the car, a low-slung, under- powered, high-geared luxury machine designed for the autobahns of Europe, not for sand, rock, brush, the Sonoran wasteland.

We park in the shade of a saguaro cactus. The shadow of the cactus is twenty feet long, one foot wide. Not much of a cooling factor. But the early December sun is far down in the southwest sky, generating more light than heat. We get out, walk over the gravel slopes, looking at the black shadows in the folds of the mountains. Those mountains begin about four miles off, but in the harsh, vivid light they seem close enough to touch, with the false clarity and dramatic exaggeration of a stage set. A fake and surreal simplicity.

My friends, perennial city dwellers from southern California, are impressed by the silence. The silence, like the visual setting, seems unreal. Overdramatic. Contrived. We talk about it, dispelling the silence in our immediate neighborhood, for a radius of a hundred feet or so. But when we pause in our conversation the silence is there again at once, complete, centered in our minds. An absurd stillness. And beyond the immediate neighborhood extends the larger neighborhood, without any human neighbors, about one hundred miles by air to the first human habitation on the east, a little Arizona mining town. Nobody lives out here. Or out there. Nobody human.

Not much water—that's the problem.

But I've got this old Kelty backpack leaning against the car, and inside the pack are maps, a sleeping bag, enough food for ten days, my old black cooking pot, matches, my wooden spoon, aspirin and Demerol, a wool shirt, a poncho, some extra pairs of socks. And some other things: a one-gallon canteen, full of water. My harmonica, of course; and Dr. Cutter's snakebite kit: I've had it for twenty years and I don't know whether it works or not.

I'm going to walk from here to that mining town beyond four ranges of desert hills. Not over the hills—too much work—but through them, where there are passes, and around them, where there are not. When I get there I'll telephone my wife; she'll pick me up by car. Such is the plan. Subordinate plans, alternate plans, and contingency plans, if needed, will be improvised on the trail.

The name of the mining town, unlikely though it seems, is Bagdad. The name of my bus stop was Why. Without the question mark.

On the bus my seatmate was an old black man from Houston, Texas, bound for Oakland, California. Looking out our big window at the desert, he said, "Ain't nothin' much out there."

I was looking too. Somewhere about thirty, forty miles to the north, beyond the foreground of cactus, creosote brush and sand, lay the route I planned to follow back.

"Ain't nothing at all out there," I said. I wanted to reinforce his opinion. "Nothing but nothing."

He nodded, smiling.

In the double seat in front of us was a black woman and her four children. A little girl with her hair braided in cornrows, with an elaborate set of strings and beads attached—like Cleopatra—looked back at us, smiling at my ridiculous beard. She said, "Where you goin'?" I said, "Home."

🕊

My friends and I build a fire with dead sticks from a nearby ironwood tree. Ironwood is slow growing, dense, very hard. A chunk from the heart of it will sink in water. We drink some beer. As the fire dies down we lay three T-bone steaks directly on the red coals, aboriginal style. They begin cooking themselves right away, no hesitation. We open and heat three cans of corn at the edge of the fire.

The sun goes down. The air between us and the near mountains becomes visible as a medium, a substance, a thing in itself, transparent but clearly four miles thick. The new, waxing moon, first quarter phase, shaped like a shield, hangs in the sky at approximately the same point occupied by the sun when we first stopped here.

We eat supper. Drink a little more beer. I produce a half pint of Jim Beam from the side pocket of my pack. We drink it, passing the bottle around the fire as the moon grows brighter, the evening more violet.

Moonlight and bourbon. The plan *was* that the three of us would camp here tonight and in the morning my friends would start driving back to California and I would start walking east toward Bagdad. One hundred and twenty miles by jeep trail, give or take a league, a mountain range now and then.

But now the plan begins to seem absurd. Unnecessarily rigid. Why wait till morning, suggests the moon? Start at once, says the whiskey percolating through the purring storage cells of my brain.

We finish the Beam. Shake hands, squeeze shoulders, kid around as I hoist the pack onto my back and pick up an extra gallon of water in a plastic jug. A final salute and I march off, the two men by the fire staring after me, silent with envy. Why aren't they coming too? Because they were not invited. "I vaunt to be alone," said Greta Garbo.

A half mile from my friends I pause and give them my parting wolf howl, then a snatch of song from *Madame Butterfly. Un bel dì* . . . He will return. Ah yes! But not just yet. Cruel of me to flaunt my joy and pride. But I can't help it. I feel like Antaeus returned to earth. The power of the desert, of the planet, surges like electricity up through my boots (Vietnam-style jungle boots, old and worn) to heart and head and out through song into the moony sky, completing the circuit.

Marching on, north, I follow this condemned jeep road as it meanders toward the mountains. Why do I *do* this sort of thing?

I don't know. I've been doing this sort of thing for thirty-five years and still don't know why. Don't even care why. It's not logical—it's pathological. We go on and on, our whole lives, never changing, repeating ourselves with minor variations. We do not change. Bruckner spent his life writing the same symphony nine times, trying to get it just right. Seeking perfection, Mozart wrote his single symphony forty-eight times. We cannot change. Saul on the road to Damascus, struck by the lightning of revelation, turns his coat inside out, drops the S and adds the P, and goes right on. Right on fantasizing. And here I am on the old devil's road to Bagdad. Under a clear sky. Marching. Singing. Marching.

Tramp . . .

Tramp . . .

Tramp tramp tramp . . .

Report the details. On my right stand the granite hills, bare except for scattered clumps of limber bush and brittlebush. Around me grow the forty-foot columns of saguaro cactus; the ironwood trees lining the dry and sandy wash; the ubiquitous creosote bushes spread out in uniform array, keeping their fixed intervals between one another; the ocotillo lifting spidery, thorny branches into the air; the barrel cactus; the hedgehog cactus; the variant brands of cholla cactus—buckhorn, staghorn, chain fruit, teddy bear. Their thick bristling limbs gleam in the moonlight, blond, beguiling, dangerous.

There is no sound but the crunch of boots on the sandy lane. And heavy breathing. The sweat drips from my hair down past my ears, from forehead into eyebrows and from there down around the corners of my eyes and along the nose. Early December, at night, a thousand feet above sea level, and I am sweating. But then my head always sweats a lot. My brains sweat. I stop, remove my hat, tie a bandana around my brow, replace the hat and go walking on. Still sweating.

My pack, loaded, weighed only thirty-five pounds on the bathroom scale at home. Since then I've added two gallons of water—sixteen more pounds. So I'm carrying one-fourth my body weight. Should not be an excessive load.

What does a man think of, alone at night, marching forward, dreaming backward? Only of conventional things: the women I have known and loved; my three superior children (superior to their father); the children of my mind and notebooks, both those born and those still paring fetal fingernails in the limbo of creation.

They give me something to look forward to. A future even better, from my personal viewpoint, than the past. The worse the world appears to become, with our industrial civilization sinking deeper into its misery and squalor, drifting toward universal civil war, the better and happier my personal life becomes. A curious inverse correlation there, disturbing to my sense of justice. What have I done to be so lucky? It stirs up fear of hubris. I have nightmares of interrogatories, G-2 colonels from the Guatemalan air force trained at Langley, Virginia. Those routine procedures down in Mexican police headquarters. I fear pain but think I could endure their worst; it is the thought of the torture of those we love that is unendurable. And we know what is happening in the Latin south, right now, only a few hundred miles away. Financed by the U.S. taxpayer. Creeping closer year by year.

"For the love of God, Montressor!" Enough of this. This is a pleasure trip. A walk through the desert hills, into my dry Elysium, under the merciful stars. Think positive, man.

A barbed-wire fence stretches across my path. The old road crosses a cattle guard. On each side of the gateway is a metal sign, red on white, one in Spanish, one in English, each adorned with a skull and crossbones—

¡AVISO!

WARNING!

USAF Gunnery Range. Unlawful to enter without permit of the installation commander. (Sec. 21, Internal Security Act 1950, 50 USC 797.) Equipment, ammunition, scrap and bomb fragments are U.S. Government property. Do not remove. Unauthorized personnel found in this area are subject to arrest and search.

I'd been warned of this, it's no surprise; the boundaries are drawn clearly on the maps. Furthermore the signs are old, riddled with rusty bullet holes. At least a few other sportsmen have been here before me, looking for the whitetail deer, the javelina, the bighorn sheep, something to kill, perhaps eat, maybe stuff and mount on the wall. Each in due season. I step across the iron rails of the cattleguard, the trench beneath half filled with blow sand, and resume my stride. Second wind, desire, the inertia of movement carry me forward.

For another hour, another two or three miles. Until the half moon, my silent time clock in the sky, touches the western horizon and I feel I've earned my rest. I choose a pretty nook hidden from the trail, scoop shallow holes for hipbones and shoulder blades in the soft sand and make my bed for the remainder of the night. Three aspirins washed down with plenty of water head off the hangover. I dream of black helicopters but sleep like a baby.

Morning, red skies of dawn. The plaintive bleat of one phainopepla off in the bush. I rise, piss, drink more water, eat an orange. My legs and feet feel as if I'd walked ten miles last night, but the same craggy hills, the same desert mountain range, rise two or three thousand feet on my right. Have to get around that range before I can start bearing east toward my goal. More harsh-looking mountains, bluish with haze and distance, lie to the north, impossibly far away.

I don't know where I am. It looks new and it all looks alien, an antique and empty land. I eat another orange—the heavy stuff first. Lighten that load. There's a bit of muscle kink between my neck and clavicles. Not good, so early in the walk. I'm not in shape, but then I never am.

Nevertheless I feel good. Tough, exalted, unstoppable. March on. My booted feet obey, returning to the jeep trail, over the rippled dunes, around the cactus, bursage, brittlebush, *Bursera*—an "elephant tree"—ten feet high, voluptuously plump at its base but tapering to a tiny tip. My feet reach the stony track and turn northward.

I can see that I've only a mile to go before I round this first range. The hills are lower now, sinking steeply into the sloping plain surrounding them. These desert mountains stand half buried in their own debris; the structural base is thousands of feet below. What we see are the high ridges and summits, as the Alps might look if inundated with a flood of sand.

Basin and range, valley and hills. A layer of mist floats above the dry lake bed on my left, motionless, veiling the next range to the west. It was a slightly dewy night; there was frost on my sleeping bag when I awoke. Must have rained in this area a few days ago. A reassuring thought. There should be water in the *tinajas*, the natural stone tanks or basins in the hills, which offer the only water, except for three man-made wells, in the hundred miles before me. I pause to drink liberally from the plastic jug in my hand. Better by far to carry that water in my belly where it'll serve a useful function (survival). Five quarts left.

Sunlight on the western peaks. Clouds in the south. Flies, beetles, lizards. No vultures; they've all gone south to Acapulco and Cancún and Puerto Vallarta for the winter. They'll be happy there.

I arrive at the terminus of the first range. Th[...] this and the second range is half a mile wide. [...] map there should be, close ahead, a junction [...] jeep trail—El Camino Diablo ("the Devil's [...] through that pass to the east, to Pozo Nuevo ("New Well"), across Mohawk Valley to the Pinto Range, across the seven-mile-wide Malpais ("Bad Land") Lava Field to the O'Brian Hills, from there to Pozo Viejo ("Old Well") and the Sweetwater Mountains (where there is a spring far off of my route) and the Charlie Bell Mountains, Gray's Well, the Pinnacle Mountains and, finally, the little burg of Bagdad, where my trail rejoins the highway.

But I find no such road junction. I walk on and on, under my pack, under the rising sun, into the heat of the open desert, clear across the opening between the mountains, but discover no trace of any so-called, alleged and no doubt mythical Devil's Road. Only my own road, devilish enough in itself, leading on north along the western slope of the next range.

Time for a halt and serious map study. I park my load and myself beneath the shade of a big ironwood tree, eat an early lunch of banana flakes and raw peanuts, drink the last of my first gallon of water and unroll the topographic maps.

Beautiful, precisely drafted, usually reliable, my United States Geological Survey maps convince me, gradually, that the hills I'd followed last night and this morning are not the hills I thought they were but a mere satellite range to the Gran Cabezon ("Big Head") Mountains, my first important objective, where the first well is. It is the Gran Cabezon, not these petty foothills, that I must traverse before I reach the Devil's Road junction.

Rather an awesome discovery. Those mountains ahead are the same that had appeared, three hours ago at dawn, to be "impossibly far away." Remote among the distant peaks stands the dark volcanic dome of the Cabezon, surmounting lighter formations of granitic rock. Somewhere beyond that dome and the farther lesser peaks, northeast of them all, should be—has got to be—

ᴊzo Nuevo, the first reliable source of water on my journey. I must hope it is reliable. My maps show three *tinajas* between here and there, which may or may not contain water. They are called Buck Tank, Cabeza Tank and Tule Tank. Each is far off my trail, up in the canyons that penetrate the flanks of the range. The Stone Tanks are in the mountains on the west—wrong direction.

And how far is Pozo Nuevo? With the aid of the map's mileage scale and a piece of string I calculate the distance from where I sit, near the nameless pass, to the well as about twenty miles. Not an impossible distance but far enough. I have one gallon of water left, two more oranges.

We are committed, my legs and I; there is no point in turning back. I shoulder the pack, resume the trek, the trudge. The step-by-step progress into what will seem for hours like an infinite regress. I wanted sweet intimacy with the desert; I've sure found it now. Each pebble on the road, each little drift of sand, each gopher hole and anthill presents itself as a trivial but unavoidable problem, requiring attention. Why?

Because this organism, this body in which I am currently housed, is not behaving properly. My feet, for example. I own a pair of good big tough feet, but these old jungle boots, size eleven, regular width, which have always seemed so comfortable and accommodating—I've had them for two years—are beginning to pinch my little toes. Under the weight of the pack and the water my feet are flattening, spreading, and my toes are getting cramped. As always, as everywhere in life, it is the little ones who suffer most. I realize now what I should have thought of earlier, that I have never before worn this pair of boots on a long-distance backpacking trip.

Never mind. I can always cut open the toes of the boots if the discomfort becomes extreme. For the present I've got a more interesting problem. My left hip joint hurts. Arthritically. That could be serious, and for the first time I feel a trace of anxiety.

Nothing odd here; the first day on the trail is often the worst. Routine shakedown. Time to measure a mile. I start counting my paces, one, two, three, four. . . . Let's see now, 5,280 feet to a mile, three feet each pace, that's one thousand seven hundred and sixty paces each and every mile. I count as far as forty strides before losing interest in the game.

A huge antelope jackrabbit springs from hiding ten feet before me, goes bounding on an arc, with thumping energy, into the cactus and creosote brush beside the road. The black-tailed mule-eared wall-eyed lagomorph. Not a rabbit at all, to be precise, but a hare. And I am the tortoise. We'll see who gets first to Pozo Nuevo, Jack. Nimble legs but thimble brain. Some coyote, God's dog, *Canis latrans*, will crunch those thews and break that frantic neck before day is done.

One mile farther and another jackrabbit leaps from its camouflage, bouncing into oblivion. As regular as mileposts, these jackrabbits, and I never spot them till they move. Haven't got my father's eye. That man could spot a rabbit sitting behind a bush, could see the liquid eyeball, the quivering form about to break and run, and he'd aim his .22 and pot the little bugger through the head, saving the meat for eating, not for shotgun pellets. My father was not a sportsman. Not a recreational shootist. He was a hunter. My mother canned the rabbit stew in bulk. It helped us through seven or eight Depression winters. Along with poached venison (the best kind).

Thus I divert myself, walking along mile after mile in my pinching boots (*pinché cabrón*, as the Mexicans say), my pack bearing down through the waist strap against my aching left hipbone.

Time for protein, a deep guzzle of water. Lessen that weight. I rest in the shade of another ironwood, pull off hat, wipe sweat from head and neck, open pack, eat my peanut butter sandwiches, drink a pint of the blessed, cool, indispensable water.

A stillness hangs in the air. Hints of rain in the pale overcast. No fighter jets in the sky. Yet. The boys must be taking the morning off. Or doing their classroom exercises, perhaps. I don't want to be caught out here in the open. I drink more water, close the pack, rise and hobble on.

Thinking about water. Buck Tank is a couple of miles to my right, hidden somewhere among those low hills. There might be water there. But it's off my route; I want to get within striking distance of Cabeza Tank by sundown. There should be water there. I know that I'm not going to reach Pozo Nuevo today. Or tonight. Not at this limping gait forced on me by unforeseen weaknesses. Like the crimp between my shoulders, this fifty-pound pack is a pain in the neck.

Forget it. I think of another walk I used to take, in Manhattan, every night for three weeks, from a hospital on Ninety-second Street—where I watched my young wife dying—to my brother-in-law's apartment building on Thirty-fifth Street. Fifty-seven blocks, about three miles. I was seeking sleep through physical exhaustion, hoping a mugger would accost me so that I could kill him. (I carried a piece, a .45 automatic, under my coat.) But the muggers are never around when you need them. Or maybe the look on my face scared them off.

Grim thoughts for a recreational stroll. Change the subject again. Look at that coyote scat on the road—neat little twists of fiber, rodent fur, tiny toenails. There goes another jackrabbit, lean and scared. Another phainopepla perches on the top of the next tree, the only type of bird I've seen so far. Black in silhouette, it resembles a Seri Indian sculpture—sleek, smooth, rigid as ironwood. Which is the wood the Seris use. The bird cries once and takes off, showing its white wing bars. It flies in fluttering fashion, wings beating hard but making slow progress as if it were learning how flying is done, to the top of a creosote bush away from the road. It watches me walk by.

The sweat drips down my ears and neck. I remove the head-band bandana without stopping and exchange it for the dry one in my hip pocket. Why does my head sweat so much, even on a relatively cool day like this? Perhaps because thinking, even the idlest kind of reminiscence, is hard for my damaged brain. (Damaged by life.) "The brain secretes thought," said a Frenchman—la Mettrie?—"as the liver secretes bile." A nice thought. As a computer generates heat. The brain perhaps is nothing but a giant sweat gland.

Now I hear the air force jets, howling like pteranodons as they swoop and climb through the sky. But they are so far away, or so high, that I cannot see them. There is the sound of aerial gunnery—a shuddering cough—from time to time. And then the screams of metal and motors fade quickly away. Instant battle, instant victory or death. Combat in the air, the last relic of knighthood. Where the sportsmen hunt each other, as they should. If only our modern wars could be limited to that sort of sporting contest. But they're not. I once heard a bomber pilot in a bar speak of his satisfaction in soaring far above what he called "that gunk downstairs."

One of their targets gleams a mile away in the valley, a twelve-foot silvery arrowhead stuck nose down in the sand. I've seen them close up—the foil-coated fins gashed and slashed by .50-caliber machine-gun bullets, the tow cable draped on a nearby bush, fragments of wood and aluminum scattered about. My practice is to set them afire and burn them flat; I consider them eyesores, these arrows fallen from the blue void.

🏃

Your left.
Your left.
You had a good home but you left.

✔

Why do I do this? (My feet hurt.) Why? Well, it's the need, I guess, for some sort of authentic experience. (My hip joint hurts.) As opposed to the merely synthetic experience of books, movies, TV, regular urban living. (My neck hurts.) To meet my God, my Maker once again, face to face, beneath my feet, beyond my arms, above my head. (Will there be water at Cabeza Tank?)

✔

This is going to be one bloody long march. The new moon hangs above El Cabezon. Pale half wafer in a clouded sky. My moving shadow angles before me, stretching toward late afternoon, toward evening. Obsessive repetition, the thinking man's beset- ting vice. Every day, lifting that awful sun into the sky, then the heavy moon. Every morning pulling on your pants, first one leg and then the other. Every night, lying down to die for a while. Every morning pulling on your pants again. Obsessive repetition. Writing the same symphony nine times (ten actually), as Bruck- ner did, better each time. And then departing from us, sweet Anton, before you got that final *finale* down on paper. Taking it into ASCAP heaven with you, where only angels could learn the score.

Marchons, marchons . . .

✔

I seem to be lying on the ground. I seem to have been sleeping. My head rests on my pack and my hat is over my eyes. A weary fly buzzes near my beard, searching, in a halfhearted manner, for edible matter. Bread crumbs, bacteria, saliva. The air is chilly, I feel cold, the day seems nearly gone and, sure enough, sitting up I see that the sun is touching the serrated edge of the western hills.

Let's make supper while there's still warmth in the air. I gather sticks from the nearest ironwood, scrape a depression in the sand, build a little squaw fire, heat water in the blackened billycan, make first a mug of Twining's tea and then a pot of Lipton's Dried Chicken Noodle Soup, lapping it up with my wooden spoon. Excellent soup. Heart-warming tea. One quart left in the old government-surplus Forest Service canteen. (There better be water at Cabeza Tank.) I eat some longhorn cheese and Verdi's salami for strength, my last carrot for fibrous bulk and good night vision. Vladimir and Estragon, I recall, ate a carrot while waiting for . . . what's his name? Godot. The carrot is a good substantial tuber. Endorsed not only by Samuel Beckett but also by Bugs Bunny.

I check the map in the waning light. Still a hard three miles to the turnoff for Cabeza Tank. On my knees, I get under and into the harness of my pack—that incubus, that malignant tumor, that block of pig iron between my shoulder blades—and stagger to my feet, groaning and grumbling like a camel with its load. One flogs oneself into movement.

The feet hurt most at each beginning, but after the first hundred paces you become accustomed to *that* source of pain; it's part of the routine. Other pangs more demanding—clanking hip joint, the knotted muscles of the back—file claims on your attention. I must get myself a camel. Or a burro, a llama, an alpaca, a Sherpa, a yak, a wheelbarrow?

We march on, yard by yard, rod after rod, into the twilight of the desert. The road has taken me among the smaller hills of the Cabezon Range, into a lonesome valley of lavender shadows, solitary saguaros with upraised, pleading arms, eroded granitic cliffs containing shallow caves that resemble the eye sockets of a skull. One owl hoots in the stillness, a great horned owl by the sound of it, although as usual the location of the cry cannot be easily determined. Predatory ventriloquism at work: such elusiveness must be disconcerting to the cottontail bunny couched in its form of dead grass under the creosote bush, tempting the rabbit to break and run for what it hopes might be a safer place. Suicide, of course: the rabbit's loss of nerve is exactly what the owl is waiting for.

I come to a dim trail junction in the sand and stone. An unmarked road leads eastward into the heart of the mountains, if these mountains have a heart. This should be, must be, the short spur road to Cabeza Tank. I am within three miles, then, of probable water.

Close enough. I go down on my knees, like a camel, and unharness myself from the painful no-longer-to-be-borne insupportable cross on my back. Unpack, lay out poncho, pad and sleeping bag, brush the dried saliva from my teeth, drink the last of the water, sit down on my bed and slowly, painfully, carefully remove the dusty boots from my cramped feet. Pull off pants and ease myself, creaking and complaining, into the nursery of my bag. Relief at last. I note the moon, low on the west, and great Orion bestriding the night sky like a colossus, and then I fade—going, going, going, gone. . . .

⊭

I wake to a cloudless dawn. Little birds cheep, chirp, warble in the chilly air. I'd gladly lie and listen for a while, prone in my sack, but a full bladder forces me out and up into the world of contingency. I shuffle barefoot over the stones, pee on a clump of cryptogams—strange wedlock of lichen and algae—and watch their furry leaves exfoliate and turn temporarily green, tricked by my golden stream into their preprogrammed response to rain. A crude joke, but it won't hurt them; in this heavily alkaline soil a gentle shower of uric acid might even strike them as curiously refreshing.

No water for morning tea. My situation is desperate but not serious. I do not panic. Calmly I breakfast on fig newtons and peanuts—it's all one to me. Sitting on my bedroll I inspect my sore feet. No blisters yet, but the little toes have been severely punished. Time for surgery. I open my knife and cut a short slit in the outer side of the toes of my boots. That should help, though it means increased vulnerability to cactus. Must keep the eyes open for cholla joints rooted to the sand and the sneaky snaky little pencil cactus hiding inside shrubs of bursage.

I repack my bag and cache it in the branches of a paloverde tree. With peanuts in my pockets and two empty water containers in hand I take the old trail road to what I hope is Cabeza Tank. If there is no water I'll be in trouble. But all the signs are good: the clear rain-washed air, yesterday's morning mist above the valley floor, the indications of recent flooding in the drainages, the yellow blossoms on the brittlebush, the bright green of the creosote, the general happiness of the birds. And my own need.

🗶

Walking along, I step on an empty shell casing half buried in the sand. A small gray lizard scurries out. He's been sleeping in there, like a wino in a culvert. I notice other artifacts of advanced technology: target fragments and more machine-gun rounds, including duds still loaded with powder and bullet. Blue bullets, Teflon-tipped—armor piercing. And over there lies a rocket assembly, a tangle of wiring spread around it like spaghetti. But this spaghetti is color coded and copper cored.

We walk on at a sprightly pace, my feet and I, relieved of our burden of yesterday. My feet feel good for a change, and there is no ache in the hip joint now. Maybe I've recovered from yesterday's twinge of arthritis. I slept on higher, drier ground last night, avoiding the sandy wash.

No sound of military jets this morning. Well, it's Sunday. The boys are in church, no doubt, praying for peace while hoping for war. Hoping for combat, action, promotions, medals—who can blame them. Must be frustrating as hell preparing for work that fails to come.

Little gray titmice flit from bush to bush with a sound like the purring of cats. Dark bunches of mistletoe cluster in the palo-verde and ironwood trees, sucking the sap of life from their patient hosts. Like ticks on a hound dog, ornamental but dysfunctional; like crab lice on a lover. Like literary critics fastening upon a defenseless author.

My road winds through a splendid cactus forest, climbs to a low divide between the hills, descends into a rocky multicolored canyon. Rock the color of raw liver, of rusted iron, of moldy sponge cake, of verdigris. Walls painted with masses of lichens in green, gray, yellow, orange, blue. Here and there a plump, stout elephant tree flourishes its golden skin and mint-green miniature leaves. Lechuguilla agave stands on the ridgeline, tall dried flower stalks tapering into the air. How do any living things survive in this barren stone and moistureless air, under the shocking light and through the dead dry stunning heat of the desert's six-month summers? The first answer is that few things do. And those that do survive by stratagem: frugality, dormancy, simplicity and, in the case of the cactus, by advance preparation—water storage.

I walk through the absolute silence for a while. No sound but the buzzing of a fly. Spiders go ballooning overhead in their pale filaments of gossamer, shining in the sunlight. I veer from the old jeep trail, or wagon road, whatever it was a century ago, to follow a game path winding through brush and down into a cool, shaded, ragweed-infested gulch. Always risky to leave the road in unknown territory, but this appears to be a shortcut.

Little heart-shaped hoofprints appear in the sand—deer? bighorn sheep? The prints are too vague in the soft sand for me to identify. Only one animal remains conspicuous in this region, by its absence—the cow. How delightful it is to walk for mile after mile without encountering the dung, the filth, the heavy tracks, the overgrazed devastation, the swarms of flies, the bovine faces and shambling forms of those gregarious brutes. I give thanks again for the United States Air Force.

Eat less beef. Of course, if I owned a cattle ranch I'd feel differently. I wish I did. But I don't. Nothing but woodsmen, peasants and vagabonds in my ancestry. But finally, after centuries of effort, we've worked our way into the lower-middle class. Free at last!

Another brittlebush in flower; bright yellow against a field of brown. A handful of rainwater shines in a cavity on top of a boulder. A rufous-throated hummingbird comes near, investigating the red bandana around my neck, then swoops away. More tracks show on the sand—the fingerlike toes of a raccoon. I find the long-discarded antlers of a deer, the tines unbranched—whitetail. Above on the hillside stands a dead saguaro with drooping limbs; it looks like a scarecrow. I pass a hummingbird bush and it too is in bloom, small red flowers like teardrops depending from each branch.

The gulch opens into a broad canyon. The slopes are covered with the blue-black stones of volcanic basalt. Small lizards cling to the rocks, heads twitching as they watch me pass. The lizards are also blue-black. Protective coloration. Darwin was right. I study my map, then follow the narrow path across a level bench of black stone. I come to a place where someone, maybe centuries ago, piled the loose rocks to form a circular wall a foot high and five feet in diameter. This is what anthropologists call an Indian sleeping circle, a windbreak. Walking long distances in winter, the ancient travelers through this region needed protection from the chilly winds; they carried no sleeping bags in those days. Nor much of anything else except a bag of parched corn, a skin or gourd for water, some articles for trade and a weapon. The remains of the windbreak, and the numerous trails in the area leading into the side canyon before me, suggest that I am approaching water.

The path leads among black boulders. On the flat panel of one are petroglyphs, cryptic symbols pecked into the hard rock by patient labor, long ago. The most prominent picture represents something like an X or cross inside a circle.

Naturally I wonder if the sign refers to water. Probably it does. But no one knows for sure anymore.

This little canyon goes uphill, into the heart of the range, straight to the base of Cabezon Peak itself; I can see that dark head two thousand feet above, resting on its pale shoulders of granite.

I pass a few of the lower stone basins, full of dampish sand. We're getting close. Then I see the shine of water oozing down a face of rock, a little drop-off twelve feet high, and know that I've arrived. I scramble up over the lip, canteen clattering, and reach the first of the natural tanks, a smooth and rounded basin holding, like a jewel, a dark amber pool of water.

I do not drink immediately but squat on the shady side of the *tinaja* and rest. The actual presence of water frees me from any sense of urgency. There is time to wait, to catch my breath, to cool off and contemplate. The pool is about two feet deep, four feet long and wide. More water than I could drink in a month. A few honeybees are sipping at the water's edge, and others are swimming in circles, trapped, on its surface. Some dove feathers float on the water. I rescue the drowning bees with a stick, fill my canteen, take a drink. It tastes sweet, cool, very good.

I leave my canteen in the shade and climb farther up into the ravine to inspect the higher tanks. There is no spring here, not even a seep; the basins that I find above, like the one below, are half filled with trapped rainwater. These are water *pockets*, not springs. In a prolonged dry season they will evaporate, dry up, though maybe not completely.

Above the pools, with a view of them all, is a shallow cave in the face of the canyon wall. The floor of the cave is covered with the ovoid pellets of bighorn sheep droppings. Lying here, the sheep would have a view of the pools and a long view up and down the canyon, the kind of vantage place much favored by these reclusive beasts. I sit for a time to share their point of view. I share the satisfaction they must feel in resting here, an assured supply of water only steps away, and safety, if only temporary, from their enemies. Of course, the bighorns could not stay in this one place; there is not enough forage. To eat they must range for many miles among the neighboring hills and mountains, under the eye of the mountain lion—and of other hunters.

I descend. On a shelf of rock near the first *tinaja* I find more petroglyphs and also grinding holes—*metates*—drilled in the solid stone. No doubt the Indians came here not only for water but also, from time to time, to camp and hunt. For the Indians this was not a remote hideaway in a wilderness but an extension of their home; for them the wilderness was home.

Image: A Walk in the Desert Hills

I drink again, all that my belly can hold, refill my canteen and walk back the way I've come to my camp of last night. Through the desert winter—too hot in the sun, too cool in the shade. I make a late lunch of salami and cheese, nuts and raisins, drink heartily once again, shoulder the pack and lurch forward, up the trail road to the well. About ten miles to go. We'll make it to Pozo Nuevo tonight by Gawd—or bust.

The feet protest under the load, but not so painfully as before. The slits in my boots do help. The ache in my hip joint has faded away, for good, I hope. No hint yet of the wrinkle in my neck muscles. All seems in order and I march along in good spirits, feeling again the vigor, power, and indomitable optimism of my middle middle age. Prime time.

Within one half mile I'm sweating like a slave. December sweat. I stop in the lean shade of a saguaro to check the maps. The dark head of El Cabezon, cocoa brown, now stands to my southeast. Good. Eight miles to go. I tie my spare bandana around my forehead.

Onward. The road leads north through a narrow valley between the main range and its parallel outrigger of subsidiary ridges. The pale rock hills are beautiful, stark in their simplicity, unclothed by vegetation, rising at forty-five degrees from the level sands. In the desert we look upon "beauty bare"; Edna St. Vincent Millay should have been told about these places. I do not hold with those who find in geometry the essence of elegance; what Euclid and his successors fell in love with was not the world out there but the world inside—structures of the human mind. They were admiring an aspect of themselves, like Narcissus doting on his image in the pool. That's my guess. But even so, I like Miss Millay's poetry.

Six miles to go.

The sun sinks behind my left shoulder. Winter sun, edging toward the solstice. Left shoulder, creaking with its accustomed pain. Feet complaining quietly, but enduring, enduring, treading over the sand, measuring the stones, my automated feet driven forward by the will.

Four miles to go.

Another pause in the shade for a drink of water. A munch of nuts and dried fruits, cheese and sausage. Getting down to basic protein here. Fuel for the metabolical engine. Gasoline for the guts. Mass into energy. Stumble on.

My shadow wobbles to the northeast, seventy-five feet long. The sun is low, glowering in the clear southwestern sky. Whatever became of the clouds of yesterday?

The moon glows overhead like a platinum egg, waxing fatter evening after evening. I've timed this expedition perfectly, and not by chance.

Twilight comes at last, the grateful coolness. I march past the gap that leads via game path to Buckhorn Tank. Should be water there too, only half a mile off according to my map, but I've got two quarts left in my canteen, no need for a side trip. Pozo Nuevo cannot be more than three miles farther.

I emerge from this lonesome valley. I've reached the north end of the Cabezon Range. My trail comes to its junction with another jeep trail leading into vast open spaces on the east and west—Camino Diablo. There's even a survey post here, set in a cairn of stones. Culture. I kneel and remove the pack, lean it against the post. Across the flat playa to the north one mountain rises into the sky, dramatically steep sided, jagged, romantic, purple hued in the evening light—Tule Peak. It resembles a clipper ship, broadside in silhouette. Nobody lives there, of course, nobody human. "Uninhabited," as we say. As is the case with everything else for as far as my eyes can see in the desert world around me.

Twilight, silence, moon and evening star. Venus blazes down the west, one soft concentricity of light. I chew on a stick of jerky.

Drink another pint of water. One quart left.

The basic fear returns for a moment. Suppose the windmill is broken down at Pozo Nuevo? Suppose the storage tank is empty? Suppose the well's gone dry?

I drop these useless fears to stare out over the sublime wasteland again. I think, for some reason, of the young Hindu novelist I met recently in Tucson. She despises Tucson: "a crude, dull, barbarous city." (Half true.) She deplores the southwestern desert: "lifeless, empty, sterile, hostile, the reification of nullity." (Nice phrase but also only a half truth.) I suggested, in my ethno-geo-chauvinistic way, that doubtless she planned, therefore, to return to her ancestral home in Bombay. She smiled, shaking her

23

head in wonder at the foolishness of my question. India, it appears, is not the kind of place one returns to voluntarily.

I wriggle into my pack harness, grunt and grumble to my feet, and face the starry east. At last, finally, now and not before, I begin the eastward leg of my walk, the true road to Bagdad, now only eighty-five miles away.

And only two more miles to the well.

Sometime near midnight I arrive. I hear the windmill before I see it, the dry rattle of turning vanes in the breeze, the rasp of ungreased gears, the whisper of the pump shaft rising and lowering. Thank God, I sigh, the windmill functions. Soon I can see the thing, a skeletal tower of galvanized steel, the revolving wheel on top, a 500-gallon storage tank beside the tower. Nearby is a one-room shanty, long abandoned, door sagging open in the moonlight, blackness within. A wooden picnic table rests on the ground under the spare shelter of a hatchet-mutilated mesquite tree. More trees line the dry stream bed beyond. My road crosses that drainage and disappears into low hills in the east. A branch road bears to my right toward the paved highway forty miles to the south.

Coming close to well and windmill, I notice that the pump shaft is broken off, and therefore pumps no water. Not a welcome observation. Nevertheless there may still be water in that big storage tank. I thump on its heavy-gauge steel with my fist, above my head, and hear the hollow boom of emptiness. I rap the tank again at waist level. Dull thud of fullness. I walk around the tank, looking for the outlet valve, and find it locked shut with a heavy-duty, brass padlock. Most alarming—but I'm too tired to investigate further now. I drink half my remaining canteen water, brush my teeth and swallow the foam, spread out my bedroll on the picnic table and go to sleep.

I sleep uneasily, waking often in order to worry. And my dreams are complex, anxious, in no way satisfying. The night is cold and very long.

Up with another red dawn. Frozen dew crackles on my sleeping bag as I unzip and slide out of it. I build a fire and boil the last of my water; tea and fig newtons for breakfast.

A mockingbird sings in the mesquite tree. Alone but not lonely, that solitary bird makes all the world seem lonely around him. (As Thoreau would have said.)

The windmill clanks and groans, revolving to no purpose, disconnected pump shaft dangling in the air. My canteen is empty. The next reputedly reliable water source on my journey is the old well, Pozo Viejo, thirty miles northeast beyond the Tule Mountains, across the Tule Desert, across the Malpais Lava Field, past the Pinto Mountains and the Pinto Sands, beyond the O'Brian Hills. Thirty miles of arid rock under the sun and moon.

Well, I could turn back to Buckhorn Tank, the way I've come, only four miles away, and maybe fill my canteen there. But that's the wrong direction.

I stare at the big, fifteen-foot-high storage tank. There's water in there, only fifty feet from where I sit on this desiccated picnic table; there's got to be a way to get it out. I consider the hatch cover on the roof of the tank; it too is padlocked, but the hinge looks old and rusty. I rummage around the cabin, find a short two-by-four, set it upright against the wall of the tank. Standing on top of the two-by-four I can reach the steel ladder riveted to the upper half of the tank. I climb the ladder and inspect the hatch. The hinge is rusted through, broken. I hook my hands under the edge of the hatch cover and bend it up and back, using hasp and padlock for a hinge. Through the opening I see water gleaming ten feet below.

Down the steel ladder, into the cabin. I remove two stove lids from the old cast-iron cookstove inside, find a ten-foot length of baling wire, get my canteen, climb the tank again, run wire through lift-sockets of stove lids, attach my canteen by its web cloth strap to the stove lids, and lower this assembly into the fetid water. My canteen gurgles, sinks, fills. I pull the works up again, take a drink—the water tastes hard as calcium, full of sodium, unpleasantly warm—detach the canteen, attach the empty plastic jug (which I've been carrying tied to the back of my pack, for possible use such as this) and fill it also. The water is not very good, but I now have two full gallons of it.

We declare a day of rest, me and my feet. I brush my teeth with the alkaline water, air out socks, underwear, sleeping bag by draping them over creosote bushes in the full glare of the sun (solar laundry).

My plan is to resume the march in late afternoon, walk half the night or until moonset. But which way? By what route? I spread my topo maps on the picnic table and study them. The simplest and easiest procedure would be to continue on the Devil's Road through the hills, over the lava field, past the Pinto Sands to Pozo Viejo. But that is thirty miles without any known source of water. Alternately, I could leave this road and walk southeast to Mesquite Tank, four miles, from there to Round Tank, twelve miles, through Cholla Pass in the Pinto Mountains, find Dove Tank (five miles?), fill belly and canteen with water and march across the next desert valley to the O'Brian Hills, rejoining El Camino Diablo at Pozo Viejo. About forty miles by that route.

I cannot decide. I'll decide later as usual, at the last possible moment, on impulse. The fool's method, which has always worked for me before.

Wish I had a burro with me, I think, or a mule. It's this chunk of dull lead in my pack, waiting for my aching spine, that dampens the spirit. I wish I had the courage to travel light, like John Muir, with only raisins and a crust of pumpernickel in my pockets. But he was wandering in the friendly High Sierra, where brooks babble and berries ripen in the placid sunshine.

Caching pack and water, I climb a hill nearby, sit down on a slab of rock at the summit. A half-dead saguaro, blown to the ground, lies near me, its green decomposing limbs draped softly upon one another, like a dying octopus. A file of ants proceeds through the shade.

Beyond the hill is the auburn-colored desolation of the desert: stony hills, lean peaks, narrow bands of olive-drab shrubbery winding along the waterless drainages and in the distance, on all horizons, from fifty to sixty miles away, the farther ranges of blue, magenta and purple mountains, where nothing human lives or ever did. I find this a cheery, even exhilarating prospect. The world of nature is faithful and never disappoints.

I scramble down the hill, back to my temporary camp. The windmill creaks and clanks in a northwest breeze—the dying machine, useless. Poking around, I find a concrete water trough hidden in a clump of tamarisk, fifty yards from the well, connected by a buried pipe. The trough is full of water, green with algae. Under a wooden barrier is the float valve, still functioning; when I push it down, the water spurts out under gravity pressure from the big tank I had so laboriously climbed and pilfered earlier. You're a clever fellow, Abbey, but not very bright.

I lie on the table, using my pack for a headrest, and try to sleep, but my state of mild excitement will not allow me to sleep. I scribble in my notebook, eat a lunch of nuts and raisins, investigate the old cabin. Nothing in there but the stove—a rusted ruin without stovepipe—and a rusty steel cot, and on plasterboard walls the graffiti of bighorn hunters, prospectors, and Border Patrolmen looking for what they call "wets"—wetbacks, illegal immigrants from south of the line. The silly word reminds me of the heat and how to allay it. I soak my shirt and bandana in the water trough, put them on. Instant cooling. I realize that my body, though still a bit sore and tired, wants to resume the walk. The impatient, itching, twitching muscles demand action. Very well. Why not? We go.

I find myself walking down the old road that leads most directly to Pozo Viejo. Something has decided. I don't know what—my feet maybe, still bruised and tender, or that cramped muscle in my neck or the faint ache in my hip joint reminding me of possible disaster. I don't mind. This is a good way to go, too, one that will require the minimum of mental effort. Just slop along, following the ruts, feet finding the way while my eyes range ahead and the mind rambles off in all directions.

Better yet, the sun is shining on the back of my pack, where I want it to shine, rather than in the southwest corner of my right eye, and the moon, pale but gibbous, rides high in the eastern sky. Even my feet, after the first painful steps, the reluctant adaptation to renewed suffering, seem to relax and cease their complaining. The slits in the boot toes help.

I come to a grave at the side of the road, flat stones arranged in the form of a hollow Latin cross, outlining the burial mound. No name, no date, but the stones are well compacted with the dust, a century old, at least. I stop.

Good resting place here. There's a nice view of the Pinto Mountains, turning pink in the evening light through a gap in the hills before me. I remove the pack, drink the hard water from my canteen, eat a bite, change headbands—the brain, that cogitative sweat gland, continues to soak my head and hair with perspiration—and get up again, advance. My shirt, wringing wet from the water trough when I started, has dried completely, then begun to dampen again from the sweat I've generated in a mere three-mile walk.

One mile farther and I come to a second grave beside the road, nameless like the other, marked only with the dull blue-black stones of the badlands. I do not pause this time. The more often you stop the more difficult it is to continue. Stop too long and they cover you with rocks.

🦅

Sun long down. Moon overhead, an ivory shield against the velvet-blue sky, the pallid constellations. Air cool, chilly. I'm still sweating but not so much, and I keep walking. The road leads on across the valley floor, through the creosote flats.

Somewhere ahead, beyond this horizon of creosote, is the lava field. Six miles across. Then into the sand dunes. Then another clay flat and then more hills and then the Old Well. Twenty miles? Twenty-four? Keep walking; you don't know where you are.

The feet hurt but they can take it. They have no choice. My back aches a bit, but it's a tolerable, familiar, almost comfortable ache. And the hip joint has seemingly lubricated its bearings, gives me no trouble.

I see little trees off in the mist of moonshine, lining another sandy wash. One would like to shuffle off in that direction, away from the road, kneel beneath the ironwood or mesquite or paloverde, whatever it is, and lay one's burden down. Sleep. Crawl in the sack and sleep.

But we're a long way from water, twenty miles or more, and the canteen is barely half full. Must keep going, cover as much distance as possible tonight while it's cool and easy, avoid the heat of day. Tomorrow we'll rest in the shade of the trees. Forever, I tell myself. Anyone fool enough to go for a walk in the desert hills when he's not an athlete, not in prime physical condition, must expect to suffer. Justice requires no less. And in any case this walk, if we complete it, will put us back in shape. In shape for what? I ask my invisible companion. Why, he says, in shape for another sedentary furlough at home. Get yourself in good shape, then lounge around the house reading Tolstoy on "What Is Art?,"

Schopenhauer on "The World as Will and Representation," Henri de Montherlant on women, love, kindness, modesty, and Mike Royko on Milwaukee. Got to get in shape for that porch swing, man.

The road is rising. Black gargoyles of lava rock stand on my right. The road becomes stony; my feet are aware of novel, troublesome, uncertain footing. But we do not stop. This is the lava field. The real *malpais*, the sick land. Few shrubs grow here, and no trees. The road, parallel tracks of pebbles and dust, winds among cinder cones and cold fumaroles. All dormant, of course. There is no vulcanism here nor has there been, say the vulcanologists, for thousands of years. I see coyote scat on the road, the prints of little rodent feet in the dust. Those boils, warts and tumors of bluish rock out there in the moonlight shelter the usual complement of lizards, spiders, scorpions, rattlesnakes.

I pass another grave, a black mound in the shape of a cross, with date and name spelled out in stones:

NAMEER

1871

Who was Nameer and what did *he* want? No one seems to know. Histories of the region make no mention of this man. Probably another gold seeker on his way to the Sierra, bound for Bodie, maybe, or Virginia City. Many traveled (in winter only) this southerly route, the Devil's Road as migrants called it, before the railways were completed in 1879. Most of them made it.

I cast a cold eye on Mr. Nameer's grave, pausing only for a moment, and trudge on. *Trudge* is the proper word now; the steady stride I preferred across the desert flat is not possible here. I have to pick my way with care among the loose stones. A stumble with this pack on my back could sprain an ankle.

Squirrelly winds spring up, whistling briefly among the humps and hillocks of petrified lava, then die away. If I were the superstitious kind I'd think there was something more than natural out here. I'd think of the supernatural. But ghosts, goblins, phantoms, spirits and even the operatives of UFOs (Unidentified Fucking Objects) avoid the prosaic, plodding, peasant mind. They dread the empiric approach. I seldom see *anything* that *ain't there*. That dark object in the middle of the road, for example, that creature the size and shape of a horseshoe crab, that thing that bestirs itself as I come near, waddling off to disappear into a crevice in the nearest boulder pile . . . what was it? A damned soul condemned to spend eternity in the form of a helmet with legs? A baking pan with limbs? Why it's only a desert tortoise, probably. Or was it?

Moonlight, silence.

I hear the tramp of large feet, the sound of heavy breathing. I stop, hesitate, look behind me. Nothing there. I tramp on, the sounds resume. I stop again, the sounds stop. Except for the sound of heavy breathing.

I know I'm getting tired. And there is too much moonlight and silence.

We come finally, at last, it must be hours later, to a sort of natural gateway out of the lava field. The road descends, we enter the Pinto Sands. The moon hangs low in the west, silent and cold and supernaturally solemn. I wander off the road, pick out a sandy basin in the lee of a dune, and bed down for what's left of the night.

I sleep poorly, waking up several times. I don't feel good; nausea in my stomach, headache, a chill in my bones. I blame it on that water from the steel tank. *The heat is bad and the water makes men sick.* I swallow a massive dose of aspirin and vitamin C tablets and dream of better things. Kneecaps. Elbows. Bright eyes and curly hair.

Ƴ

One quart left. Nine miles to go. I add Tang to the water, making it more or less palatable, eat the last of my banana flakes—I feel no appetite for anything more—and slog on down the sandy tracks toward the O'Brian Hills, where the sun is coming up. The hills seem to recede before me, unapproachable. On my right, however, the Pinto Range swings slowly, steadily around, reveal-ing new aspects of its two-tone, laminated structure: sharp crags, deep gorges sinking into shadow, long wrinkled ridges winding toward the sunlit peaks on the crest of the range, pale granite formations thrust above planed-off brown basic andesite. The metamorphic and the igneous lie exposed to one more rising sun.

Rising sun? The sun does not rise, insist the literal minded, but, rather, the earth revolves. Really now? What is that assertion but an inference, based on a chain of inferences, linked by vari-ous and inferential astronomical calculations? Eh? Tell me, O Copernican Guru, who yet among humankind has stood back far enough from the solar system (if it is a system) to see, with naked eyeballs, in direct unmediated perception, the earth revolve, the planets rotate, around that peculiar ball of fire men call . . . Sun? Name one.

Most of what we call science is this, and no more: verified but inferential knowledge, grounded on unverifiable assumptions. "If this, then that . . ." A likely story. Probably true. But by no means certain, not in the sense that this earth beneath my feet, these hills before my sight, that sky, those clouds, those birds above are certain. I can *see* the sun rise each morning; I have never *seen* the earth rotate. Therefore I do not accept the doc-trines of science as *gospel truth* and would be a fool to do so. Why betray common sense for the sake of any theory, cult or doctrine? Why deny the truth of living experience out of deference to some body of esoteric knowledge, no matter how complex, coherent and conclusive it might seem to be?

Therefore, I repeat, the sun rises. It also rises. Every morning. I've never seen it fail. I hurl this truth in the teeth of Aristarchus, Copernicus, Galileo, Laplace, Newton (a fig for Newton!) and all their dutiful, unquestioning, leaden-eyed, sober-faced and white-smocked successors. That daisy chain of balding clones. What's the gain in ridding ourselves of the Judeo-Christian hierarchy of intellectual oligarchs if we merely and meekly accept another power-hungry ideology in its place?

"Knowledge is power," said Francis Bacon, giving the game away four centuries ago.

And power, now as always, is the natural enemy of truth. And so, I while away the miles between here and there, between sand and water, death and survival. One pint left.

The bluish peaks of the Seco Mountains rise beyond the O'Brian Hills. Perspectives change. I must be making some kind of progress, or else the earth is revolving beneath my feet.

But the feet still hurt. There's a hot spot on my left foot. Time for some more doctoring. I shed the pack, sit on a rock, remove boot and socks (I'm wearing two socks on each foot), and find the blood blister I'd been expecting. I sterilize my knife blade with a flaming match, make the incision, drain the blood and lymph from the wound, patch with two Band-Aids, put on my cleanest dirty socks, restore boot to foot (my feet live in my boots) and stagger on.

Rejoicing all the way to the grave.

The grave of Mr. O'Brian (for whom these hills were named) is another low mound by the side of the road, marked and named on my map. An iron cross, made of what look like two welded braces from a buckboard wagon, stands at the head of O'Brian's grave. I sit on the middle of it, on the old boy's stomach, and eat my lunch of cheese, walnuts, and the last of my Verdi's Italian Style Dry Salami. Excellent. I drink the last of my Tang-tinted tainted water and watch two ravens circle above, protesting my presence.

"Tok! Tok!" cry the ravens. Big, bold, intelligent birds, they suggest to me, now as before, the basic kinship of living things. I can empathize with and sympathize with the emotions of my feathered cousins above. At least I think I can, here and now, sitting on this stony grave under the Arizona sun.

The brown towhees creeping under the brush, though, pay me no mind. They couldn't care less. And the cactus wrens, chattering like ratchets in the cholla thickets. And that sudden wild whoop of coyotes off in the distance, unendurably excited, one half mile yonder down the wash, running a rabbit into a fatal circle. Good hunting, *compañeros*.

How nice to sit here on my grave, sun basking while the jet fighters scream above, miles away, shooting at their tinfoil targets, and the little black-throated desert sparrows cheep among the bursage, creosote, mesquite and cactus.

The hideous howls of the United States Air Force veer away, fading out, and the vast tremendous stillness comes sweeping back. How pleasant to be here, in the southwestern corner of a nation of two hundred and thirty million people, in the heart of the Gunnery Range, absolutely alone. Two hundred thirty million!—and nobody home but me.

"Awk!" the ravens cry. "Awk! . . . Awk! . . ."

How true, I think, how true.

I have now walked seventy-five miles plus side trips. Only fifty to go. Five days so far in the open, without roof, without walls. An emotion old as the human race, essence without name, flows through my heart and mind.

The windmill turns in the distance. Half a mile? Sunlight glints on the revolving vanes. Suppose that pump too is out of order? Suppose there is no water there?

Don't give it another thought.

Me and my feet walk on. (Hardly any tread left in these old jungle boots.) Once a foot soldier, always a foot soldier. But I'll say this much for walking: it's the one and only mode of locomotion in which a man proceeds entirely on his own, upright, as a human being should be, fully erect rather than sitting on his rear end.

And in intimate com-union with the ground. The ground of being, our only ground, this here ontological gravel, dirt, stone, sand, weeds, birdshit and coyote scat.

We pass a lollipop saguaro beside the road. A lollipop is a cactus nibbled to death around the base by rodents and rabbits, so that the poor bare bones of the plant—the woody ribs—are exposed, holding aloft the foot or two of green flesh beyond reach of the starving vermin. (Not enough coyotes.)

I walk past ragged ironwoods sick with mistletoe—those parasitic clumps of rusty brown, where lovers never yet have kissed nor likely ever will. Past man-high shrubs with little scarlet blossoms: the hummingbird bush, as I choose to call it, where sure enough a few ruby-throated and Costa's hummingbirds are buzzing about.

And then the windmill, the storage tank, the old *pozo* itself come in sight. This windmill appears to be in working order, pump shaft intact, sliding up and down. The valve at the bottom of the tank is not padlocked, and when I turn the valve handle water pours out, clear and cool, which I splash on my sweating face and then catch in the open mouth of my canteen. Feeling acutely thirsty, weak and dehydrated, I do not drink at once but sit for a while in the shade, letting my body cool before taking the first cautious sip. This water is good—soft, sweet, highly potable. I am relieved and grateful. I declare another day of rest.

In the evening, near sundown, after an early supper, I go for a stroll up a mountain path. My destination is the Mohawk Mine (abandoned), about two miles off, according to my map. As I walk, gazing at the jagged peak a thousand feet above, I am startled by a hissing noise at my feet. I halt with the quick reflex of fear. Looking down I see a fat lizard, eighteen inches long, encased in a beaded yellow-black hide, gaping up at me with drooling, moist, purple mouth. A Gila monster, poisonous but scared. Two feet from my right foot, it backs toward the loose rocks beside the trail, hissing defensively. I cannot resist the temptation to squat down and tease the little fellow with a stick. I poke it gently in the side, hoping the lizard will bite on the tip of the stick and give me a tug-of-war. But the Gila monster is more intelligent than it looks. Ignoring my prodding, it keeps its bright beady eyes fixed on me as it backs beneath the shelter of the rocks. I leave it in peace and walk on up the path to the mine.

There's nothing left but the ruins of frame shacks, a few hand-built stone walls shoring up a wagon road, remains of a mule corral, a mound of rusted cans and broken bottles, the diggings. I find several deep pits on the mountainside, one with a rotted wooden ladder descending into darkness. The smell of something ancient, stale and sick rises from the depths. I lob a couple of big stones into the hole. They crash through moldy timbers, clatter off the wall and ricochet to the bottom, followed by cascades of debris. Immediately a swarm of bats arises from the blackness, gibbering, squeaking at me.

I back off and take the antique wagon road down the hill, admiring once again the doughty labor of these old-time hard-rock miners, who worked their mines with no more technology than pick and shovel, carbide head lamps, hand-pushed ore cars and the reluctant slavery of mule, horse, burro.

The road winds east. I leave it, walking northwest through a garden of teddy-bear cholla toward Pozo Viejo and my camp for the night, guiding myself by Polaris. Something stabs me in the big toe, sharp as a serpent's tooth. In instant panic I spring aside, with the same movement trying to kick the thing loose. But it clings like the devil, not a rattlesnake or Gila monster but a furry ball of cholla cactus. I sit down and remove the spiny object using a pair of stones for tongs; the numbing, venomous pain remains. I unlace and pull off the boot and draw an inch-long needle from my toe. One drop of blood wells from the puncture. The spine has entered not through the slit in the toe of my boot but through the leather and two pairs of socks. The pain lingers, like a bee-sting. If I were writing a novel about the Wild West and wanted to punish my villain properly, I'd arrange to have him fall from a cliff into a thicket of teddy-bear cholla. The Brothers Grimm or Hans Christian Andersen or even Walt Disney could not imagine a more exquisitely fiendish death.

Elegant clouds the shape and color of salmon float against the green sky of dawn. Rose on green, heads into the wind stream. Coyotes are crying down the moon. Still lying in my sack, I hear the thud of hoofs near the water trough by the well, two hundred yards off. Antelope? Deer? Javelina? I rise and peer into the gloom but can see nothing through the brush. The sound dies away.

Breakfast: Constant Comment teabag in my one-pint GI canteen cup, floating in water that's bubbling hot. My last fig newton. My last slice of salami. My last chunk of longhorn cheese. No more crackers, no more bread. Nothing left now but raisins, nuts, jerky, dried apricots like little baby's ears—iron rations. And forty-five miles to go.

I like it here at the old well, Pozo Viejo, the water is good, the game abundant, and if I had enough food or something to hunt with I'd be tempted to linger for a few days, weeks or years. But I carry no weapon except a pocketknife and lack the ambition to fashion noose, deadfall, slingshot, spear, bow. And furthermore the usual obligations, without which a man is nothing, are calling me home.

There is no choice but to go on. On to Gray's Well, the next water hole, twenty-five miles away, and then the final twenty around the Pinnacle Mountains to the highway, Bagdad, a drink at the Copper King Bar and rendezvous with my wife. (Whom I'm beginning to miss a little, by the way, when I permit myself to think about her.)

Coyotes howling, yipping, barking, chanting in the brush this morning—that thrilling call of the wild. Like a loon's cry in the lake country, the song of the coyote, God's own beloved dog, is the voice of the desert, leitmotiv of the west.

Eating my breakfast, such as it is, I take care not to drop crumbs on the ground. Don't want to corrupt the ants. Let the little fuckers find their own food, as I did, in the supermarkets of Tucson, Arizona.

One more cup of tea. And then I drink the good sweet water from the old well, filling my belly to capacity. I am resolved today to carry no more than a single quart from here to Gray's Well. No more overload in this comparatively cool December weather. Why break my back anymore? There has got to be water at Gray's Well—a rancher named Henry Gray once lived there—and if there isn't I'll die, and what of it?

I pull on my dirty cashmere socks, and over them a pair of dirty heavy-duty lumberjack socks. Baby those feet. Load my pack, scatter the ashes of the fire, break a bough from a creosote bush and sweep away all trace of my camping here. No one will ever know.

Once more into your britches. Nobody says good-bye.
We march on.

Into the forenoon sun, thinking of coyotes. Thinking of mountain lion. Thinking of bighorn sheep, grizzly bear, pronghorn antelope, whitetail deer, javelina, coatimundi, golden eagle, redtail hawk, peregrine falcon, California condor, blackfooted ferret, gray whale, eland, elephant, zebra, giraffe, gazelle, ibex, Siberian tiger, rhinoceros, water buffalo . . . and back to the American buffalo, the bison. Most of these threatened with extinction before the end of another century.

Too bad, they say. Human expansion requires it, they say. Human progress and well-being are more important than preservation of obsolete and uneconomic species, they say. False, I say. The defense of wildlife is a moral issue. All beings are created equal, I say. All are endowed by their Creator (call that God or call it evolution) with certain inalienable rights; among these rights are life, liberty and the pursuit—each in its own way—of reproductive happiness.

I say these things because too few others will, because far too many say the opposite. Humanity has four and a half *billion* passionate advocates—but how many speak for the polar bear? for the manatee? for the crocodile? for the gray wolf? for the Bengal tiger? for the Mexican grizzly? for the iguana? for the beaded lizard? for the sperm whale? for the caiman? for the monitor? for the kangaroo? for the ring-tailed cat? for the desert tortoise? for the moose? for the native trout? for the humpback whale? for the dolphin? for the wallaby? for the koala bear? for the panda? for the caribou? for the red wolf? for the panther? for the musk-ox? for the black leopard? for the snow leopard? for the wild yak? for the mustang? for the Dall sheep? for the alligator? for the hippopotamus? for the pupfish? for the snail darter? for the harp seal? for all of the world's endangered?

It is a man's duty to speak for the voiceless. A woman's obligation to aid the defenseless. Human needs do *not* take precedence over other forms of life; we must share this lovely, delicate, vapor-clouded little planet with all. And I quote: "For I say unto you . . . , as you do to the least of these, so you do unto me. . . ."

And not only the voiceless creatures but the defenseless tribes-people too—the Indians of the Amazon, the pygmies of Africa, the Seris and Tarahumaras of Mexico, the Kurds and Kazaks and Montagnards of Asia, the Hopis and Cheyennes and Innuits of North America—they too have the right to survival. To aid and abet in the destruction of a single species or in the extermination of a single tribe is to commit a crime against God, a mortal sin against Mother Nature. Better by far to sacrifice in some degree the interests of mechanical civilization, curtail our gluttonous appetite for things, ever more things, learn to moderate our needs, and most important, and not difficult, learn to control, limit and gradually reduce our human numbers. We humans swarm over the planet like a plague of locusts, multiplying and devouring. There is no justice, sense or decency in this mindless global breeding spree, this obscene anthropoid fecundity, this industrialized mass production of babies and bodies, ever more bodies and babies. The man-centered view of the world is anti-Christian, anti-Buddhist, antinature, antilife and—antihuman.

Mumbling, grumbling, cursing and laughing, one more lunatic in a world of murderers, I walk southeast by east along the flank of the Seco Mountains and through the scattered Antelope Hills. I see no antelope, but I do catch a glimpse of three, four Sonoran whitetail deer bounding gracefully across the road fifty yards before me, their white tails up in "plume" position—alarm flags. Small, only two to three feet high at the shoulder, brownish-gray in color, they blend quickly, easily with the desert vegetation, disappearing while I watch.

I pause for a piss in the slim shade of a saguaro. With my free hand I pluck at the rigid spines on the saguaro's trunk, pizzicato.

The spines have a dull but musical tone, a little flat but each vibrating to a slightly different pitch. With sufficient patience one could learn to play a tune on the taut whiskers of a tall cactus.

The road turns northeastward, detouring around the fifteen-hundred-foot-high bulk of what the map identifies as Bighorn Mountain. It appears that I can save myself three miles of walking by taking a shortcut over the low pass between Bighorn Mountain and the last of the Antelope Hills, rejoining the jeep road out on the creosote flats of Mohawk Valley. So I turn off and follow a game path along the contour of the slope.

I'm half a mile from the road when I hear the rhythmic beat of a helicopter, the rapid shudder of rotating wings. At once, instinctively, without looking up or around, I step off a cutbank and drop into the deep shade of an ironwood tree. I lie quite still. The sound of the machine comes from the direction of Pozo Viejo, approaching swiftly. Then I see it, flying low above the road, following my route, a huge dark sleek military helicopter of the type known as a "Huey," bearing on its fuselage the markings of the United States Air Force. It passes by, vanishing north beyond the profile of Bighorn Mountain. Looking for me? Not likely. But possible. I wait. In fifteen minutes the dragon returns, still following the road, and disappears back into the west. The vibrations fade quickly into nothing, into nothingness, into the basic absurdity from which the monster came.

I wait another half hour, grateful for the shade and the excuse, scribbling seditious thoughts in an innocent little notebook, before rising to my knees, to my feet, stiff and cranky again, like a soreheaded mule. The feet as usual object to the first few steps forward, sending their signals of suffering, anguish and injustice via work gangs of ganglia to the imperial brain. Futile objections; we shamble ahead as one, the complete contrived ramshackle assembly of bone, flesh, blood, viscera, nerve, sweat gland, memory, hope, fear and perception, together with the millions of accessory organisms in our secrets and secretions that go along as they always do, apparently just for the ride.

One adjusts. Readjusts. Makes certain internal corrections and realignments, restoring trim, achieving that serial illusion of balance between the fall and the recovery, an act repeated every second in walking, which sustains in turn our automatic, cinematic notion—functionally adaptive—of progressive movement through the space-time continuum.

Everything is illusion, say my Californicated friends, their minds vaporized by the relaxed and comfortable nihilism of the mythical Orient. All is a dream. *La vida es un sueño*, et cetera.

Could be, I agree. Might be the case. You got a hold of something there, pardner, but don't stamp your brand on it yet. Could be this here illusion is real, old buddy, a real illusion, and the only one we got.

Delirium. Walking along, I realize I've forgotten to button my fly. My prick is hanging out, dangling like a banner in defeat. Like the nose cone of a possum. Like the pseudopod of an uncircumcised amoeba. Like the ENEC of an MX. But what the hell—it looks so nice out today I think I'll leave it out all afternoon. (I know they're out there, I can hear them breathing.) (Or, who was that lady I saw you with last night? That was no lady, that was your wife.) (Or, what did the wall-eyed Jean-Paul Sartre say to Albert Camus when they ran into each other in the doorway of the Café Flore? Sartre said, *Pourquoi ne regards-tu pas où tu vas, Albert?* [Why don't you look where you're goin', Albert?] And what did Albert Camus say? He said, *Pourquoi ne vas-tu pas vers ce que tu regards, J.-P?* [Why don't you go where you're lookin', J.-P?])

I am walking through a forest of giant saguaros, their tall stately fluted trunks like the columns of a Greek ruin. Unfinished ruins. Some of them have a sunburnt look—bronzed on the south side, green on the north. I see one with an arm dangling almost to the ground, like an elephant's trunk, then curving upward at the end. Six months from now these stationary creatures will be putting out clusters of creamy white flowers, like bouquets, at the tip of each limb. And the flowers will fade to make fruit, pink and fleshy as your daughter's labia. And the birds will gather the fruit, eat the flesh, scatter the seeds on the barren ground. But not utterly barren, even here. A few will germinate, sprout, take root, resume the endless, pointless, beautiful cycle, again and again and again.

For what purpose? Only the weary and the foolish insist on a purpose. Let being be. To make shade for a titmouse, that is the purpose.

Deliria. Maybe I need some shade myself. The sweat, as customary, drips down the flanges of my snout.

I come down from the pass, stumble in and out of a cross ravine, regain the jeep trail and flop down in the shelter of a friendly paloverde tree. *Blessed* coolness. I pull off the pack, set it against the tree and use it for a backrest. I drink half of my one quart of water.

Looking eastward I can see, through a misty haze, hopelessly far away across the flat open desert plain, the iron crags of Hatchet Peak. Somewhere near the north base of that particular mountain is Gray's Well—next water. Last water. Objective for tonight. Essential that I get there. Though impossibly far away.

I have now walked around three distinct mountain ranges and across two of the intervening valley floors. Basin and range country. One more basin, one more range to go.

A distant glitter, fixed on a mountainside, catches my eye. A shot-down target. Dud shells, rockets, fragments of metal and wood. And at the moment I see that point of light I also hear, overhead, cracking the sky, the abrupt *wham-BAM!* of a sonic boom. A detonation that stops the heart. And then the anguished scream, like a tortured dinosaur, of a jet plane pulling out of a violent dive, the howl pinched out by silence. I see nothing, the metal beast is too high, too far. Crash, you bastard, I'm praying. Explode. Dive once more and bury yourself forever in the talus slopes of Mount Motherfuck.

One day our prayers shall be answered.

I hear Gambel quail crooning, clucking, calling to one another down in the brush along the wash, making the reassuring humdrum noises of sanity, common sense, reason, life.

Suppose some poor pair of bighorn sheep were copulating, about to come, when that helmeted android in his flying machine broke through the barrier of sound? Might have sterilized the poor brutes forever, or worse, caused them to conceive some mutant monster of a sheep, an animal with horns of aluminum, hoofs of Bakelite, a Dacron Fiberfill coat of fleece. I'm serious. If the life of natural things, millions of years old, does not seem sacred to us, then what can be sacred? Human vanity alone? Contempt for the natural world implies contempt for life. The domination of nature leads to the domination of human nature. Anything becomes permissible. We return once more to the nightmare cultures of Hitler, Stalin, King Philip II, Montezuma, Caligula, Heliogabalus, Herod, the Pharaohs; Christ sacrificed himself in vain.

The sky is silent. My sense of outrage—volatile as gasoline—evaporates as quickly as it came. The sound of the quail, the sibilance of the air stirring the branches of the paloverde, the ancient voices of children (where did they come from?) restore my equanimity.

The sky is dark and royally blue, infinitely deep. There are no clouds. One forty-foot saguaro towers nearby, gold-green in the afternoon sun; I hear the breeze whisper among its tense whiskers. Rough and rocky hills stand on the south, dark with shadows—a hideout for erls, elves, gnomes, trolls, wizards. One shaman from the Pleistocene epoch, twenty thousand years old, squats in his cave, facing the lowering sun. Why not? No man, probably, has bothered to climb into those hills in this century, if ever. As it should be. Let us leave some places forever undisturbed.

Resting here by the side of this primitive road, beside these dim tracks winding through a landscape like that of some medieval legend, I recall the sensation though not the images of the dream in which, through which, by which I gradually awoke this morning. It was a sensation, a suffusion, of absolute well-being, a warm, buzzing, friendly, leisurely dream, refreshing as good water, deep as this sky, old as those hills over yonder, leaving with me an afterglow of sweetness and happiness that now, ten hours later, I still recall with a sense of serene delight.

What was that dream about? I can't say. What is music about? What is this paloverde, this cool shaded earth, that saguaro, those hills, that sky about? And now I am not certain, in trying to grasp the sensation, that it even *was* a dream. Indeed, it might have been the opposite—an awakening. A brief awakening that slips through my grasp, elusive as a rainbow of light, when I try to cling to it.

✦

On the road. I am far out in the center of the valley floor, near sundown. Hatchet Peak is still ten, twelve, fifteen miles away—I can't tell.

Still marching. My feet hurt but *I* feel fine. My shadow stretches fifty feet before me, draping itself over the golden sand and dried clay, over the scattered creosote shrubs. A black Pinacate beetle ambles before me, tail up, head down, as if on the spoor of something of concentrated interest. I touch the beetle with a twig, and it rolls on its back, legs splayed in mortal rigor, playing dead.

Small craterlike anthills appear in the sand of the roadway, most of them undergoing a busy expansion by their occupants. I see a pair of these little ant craters built so close together that they partly overlap; in each the ants laboriously tote grains of sand to the rim of their own crater and roll them down into the crater of their neighbor. Reminds me of New Jersey. Of California. Of Phoenix and Tucson. None of the ants seems to mind. The work goes steadily on.

As I reach the center of the valley floor, the lowest point between the parallel mountains, the old road enters a thicket of creosote tall as my head and of tangled mesquite trees burdened with mistletoe overarching the road. I smell water under the gloom. The tracks become damp, muddy, slick as silt. A narrow pool appears, filling a rut left by the last truck or jeep that passed through here. I drink the remainder of the water in my canteen and slop through mud to the edge of the pool, which is ten feet long, a foot wide, and two inches deep. The water is clear but clouds instantly with fine silt when I dip my canteen into it. No matter; the silt will settle. I fill my canteen with the muddy water and go on, around the puddles and through the dense brush until I reach dry ground on the other side of this miniature ephemeral desert swamp.

The full moon rises as the sun goes down. Hatchet Peak, like a rusted ax blade, glows dull and harsh in the final light. The temperature goes down with the sun. I button my shirt, tighten the bandana around my neck, remove the sweat-soaked bandana from around my head, push my hat down snugly and tramp on faster.

The road climbs into open desert again, into sand and rock. Land of *nada*, kingdom of *nihilo*. God knows there's plenty of both out here. But it's a positive nothingness, as an idealist would say, rich in time, space, silence, light, darkness, the fullness of pure being.

Tramp . . .

Tramp . . .

Tramp tramp tramp . . .

Amazing how these feet hold up, these legs stride on, mile after mile after mile after mile . . .

Moonlight and stillness, once again.

Fence coming up. Open gateway, cattle guard, more of the metal warning signs shot through with more primeval bullet holes. I step across the bars of the cattle guard, leaving behind the USAF Gunnery Range, entering a different division of our public lands. Six miles to Gray's Well. Hatchet Peak rises high and silent over the desert hills, mystic pale and remote, mysterious by moonlight.

Definitely weary, I stop for a while, sit on a rock and make myself a tiny fire of sticks and twigs, leaning over the flames and into the smoke to warm myself. The punky, dry-rotted paloverde sings a little tune as it burns, and I imagine I hear voices coming toward me on the road. I look up. But no, not yet, there is nobody there.

The fire dies, I rise and walk on, up a meandering narrow and stony road that twists into the foothills of my final range. At long last, well after midnight by the stars, I top a rise and see below, perhaps half a mile farther, the dull gleam of moonlight on a sheet-metal shack, the metallic vanes and the tail of a windmill.

Gray's Well. Close enough. I turn aside up a little gulch, stop near an ironwood, plant my canteen upright in the sand to let the silt settle out, spread my poncho and pad and sleeping bag on the ground, dry-brush my teeth, crawl in the sack and fall like a stone into the sea of sleep. The last thing I remember is a splendid meteor, gold fading into violet as it floats across the sky.

🕊

Awake to a cold, bleak, clouded, windy dawn. I should get up. I lie in my sack a few more minutes, though, feeling tough, mean, ornery, lonesome and horny. I think of my wife, the sweet reunion due us tonight. I think, by inevitable association, of other girls and women I have known—too many of them, I suppose, over the years, through the decades. That long and lovely chain of loves. Vanity, no doubt, to treasure those memories. But I cannot help it. They honored me with their love; I honored them with mine. Cocky as a rooster I told myself: you are an artist. An adventurer. A human man. Not some shoe clerk, knee-jerk liberal or kneepad Tory, insurance adjuster or group-encounter therapist or assistant professor of data processing at your local Vocational Tech. No androgyne with retracted balls and frightened pizzle. So I told myself, and so I believe right now, and so it has to be.

Arise. Piss. Pull on pants and boots. Build a fire. Decant puddle water, now clear, into billycan. Boil, pour in final package of beef stew, let soak, warm, coagulate. Eat, goddamn! And Mother of God, it's good! Good! Bloody good tucker, mates.

Pack on back, I walk down the grade to Gray's Well. There are several shacks here, a corral, an abandoned trailerhouse of the antique type used by sheepherders. A caretaker is supposed to live here, but I find nobody home. I fill my canteen at the well, drink deep and start up the road toward Bagdad, twenty-five miles. Already I see a dirty yellow smudge across the eastern sky: smog from the Phelps-Dodge copper smelter. I come to a junction with a graded dirt road leading north on the left. Good-bye to the jeep trail. I stride toward town feeling proud, strong, hard, happy, marching toward the highway, the telephone, the collect call home that will bring her to me at last. It's been six days and seven nights—too long.

All morning I walk, and at noon a rancher comes by in his pickup truck, stops, offers me a ride the final ten miles into town. I am much too proud to refuse the invitation. I throw my pack in the bed, climb into the cab. Seated once more on my rear end, like everybody else in the modern world, I slump with relief back into the delights of the civilization I love to despise. My feet are even happier than I am. Within minutes my 115-mile walk through the desert hills becomes a thing apart, a disjunct reality on the far side of a bottomless abyss, immediately beyond physical recollection.

But it's all still there in my heart and soul. The walk, the hills, the sky, the solitary pain and pleasure—they will grow larger, sweeter, lovelier in the days and years to come, like a treasure found and then, voluntarily, surrendered. Returned to the mountains with my blessing. It leaves a golden glowing on the mind.

TWO

HOW IT WAS

The first time I had a glimpse of the canyon country was in the summer of 1944. I was a punk kid then, scared and skinny, hitchhiking around the United States. At Needles, California, bound home for Pennsylvania, I stood all day by the side of the highway, thumb out. Nobody stopped. In fact, what with the war and gasoline rationing, almost nobody drove by. Squatting in the shade of a tree, I stared across the river at the porphyritic peaks of Arizona, crazy ruins of volcanic rock floating on heat waves. Purple

51

crags, lavender cliffs, long blue slopes of cholla and agave—I had never before even dreamed of such things.

In the evening an old black man with white whiskers crept out of the brush and bummed enough money from me for his supper. Then he showed me how to climb aboard an open boxcar when a long freight train pulled slowly out of the yards, rumbling through the twilight, eastward bound. For half the night we climbed the long grade into Arizona. At Flagstaff, half frozen, I crawled off the train and into town looking for warmth and hospitality. I was locked up for vagrancy, kicked out of jail the next morning, and ordered to stay away from the Santa Fe Railway. And no hitchhiking, neither. And don't never come back.

Humbly I walked to the city limits and a step or two beyond, held out my thumb and waited. Nobody came. A little after lunch I hopped another freight, all by myself this time, and made myself at home in a big comfortable empty side-door Pullman, with the doors open on the north. I found myself on a friendly train, in no hurry for anywhere, which stopped at every yard along the line to let more important trains roar past. At Holbrook the brakemen showed me where to fill my canteen and gave me time to buy a couple of sandwiches before we moved on.

From Flag to Winslow to Holbrook; and then through strange, sad, desolate little places called Adamana and Navajo and Chambers and Sanders and Houck and Lupton—all the way to Albuquerque, which we reached at sundown. I left that train when two rough-looking customers came aboard my boxcar; one of them began paring his fingernails with a switchblade knife while the other stared at me with somber interest. I had forty dollars hidden in my shoe. Not to mention other treasures. I slipped out of there quick. Suddenly homesick I went the rest of the way by bus, nonstop, about twenty-five hundred miles, the ideal ordeal of travel, second only to a seasick troopship.

But I had seen the southern fringe of the canyon country. And did not forget it. For the next two years, through all the misery

and tedium, humiliation, brutality and ugliness of my share of the
war and the military, I kept bright in my remembrance, as the
very picture of things that are free, decent, sane, clean and true,
what I had seen and felt—yes, and even smelled—on that one
blazing afternoon on a freight train rolling across the Southwest.

I mean the hot dry wind. The odor of sagebrush and juniper, of
sand and black baking lava rock. I mean I remembered the sight
of a Navajo hogan under a bluff, red dust, a lonesome horse
browsing far away down an empty wash, a windmill and water
tank at the hub of cattle trails radiating toward a dozen different
points on the horizon, and the sweet green of willow, tamarisk
and cottonwood trees in a stony canyon. There was a glimpse of
the Painted Desert. For what seemed like hours I could see the
Hopi Buttes, far on the north, turning slowly on the horizon as
my train progressed across the vast plateau. There were holy
mountains in the far distance. I saw gleaming meanders of the
Little Colorado and the red sandstone cliffs of Manuelito. Too
much. And hard-edged cumulus clouds drifting in fleets through
the dark blue sea of the sky. And most of all, the radiance of that
high desert sunlight, which first stuns then exhilarates your
senses, your mind, your soul.

But this was only, as I said, the fringe. In 1947 I returned to the
Southwest and began to make my first timid, tentative explora-
tions toward the center of that beautiful blank space on the maps.
From my base at the University of New Mexico, where I would
be trying, more or less, for the next ten years, off and on, to win a
degree, I drove my old Chevy through mud and snow, brush and
sand, to such places as Cabezon on the Rio Puerco and from there
south to Highway 66. They said there was no road. They were
right. But we did it anyhow, me and a lad named Alan Odendahl
(a brilliant economist since devoured by the insurance industry),
freezing at night in our kapok sleeping bags and eating tinned
tuna for breakfast, lunch and supper. Tire chains and skinned
knuckles; shovels and blisters; chopping brush to fill in a boghole,

I missed once and left the bite of the ax blade in the toe of my brand-new Red Wing engineer boots. (In those days philosophy students wore boots; now—more true to the trade—they wear sandals, as Diogenes advised, or go barefoot like Socrates.) Next we made it to Chaco Canyon, where we looked amazed at Pueblo Bonito in January. And then to the south rim of Canyon de Chelly—getting closer—and down the foot trail to White House Ruin. An idyllic place, it seemed then; remote as Alice Springs and far more beautiful.

On one long holiday weekend another friend and I drove my old piece of iron with its leaky gas tank and leaky radiator northwest around the Four Corners to Blanding, Utah, and the very end of the pavement. From there we went by dusty washboard road to Bluff on the San Juan and thought we were getting pretty near the end of the known world. Following a narrow wagon road through more or less ordinary desert we climbed a notch in Comb Ridge and looked down and out from there into something else. Out *over* something else. A landscape that I had not only never seen before but that did not *resemble* anything I had seen before.

I hesitate, even now, to call that scene beautiful. To most Americans, to most Europeans, natural beauty means the sylvan—pastoral and green, something productive and pleasant and fruitful—pastures with tame cows, a flowing stream with trout, a cottage or cabin, a field of corn, a bit of forest, in the background a nice snow-capped mountain range. At a comfortable distance. But from Comb Ridge you don't see anything like that. What you see from Comb Ridge is mostly red rock, warped and folded and corroded and eroded in various ways, all eccentric, with a number of maroon buttes, purple mesas, blue plateaus and gray dome-shaped mountains in the far-off west. Except for the thin track of the road, switchbacking down into the wash a thousand feet below our lookout point, and from there climbing up the other side and disappearing over a huge red blister on the earth's surface, we could see no sign of human life. Nor any sign of any kind of life, except a few acid-green cottonwoods in the canyon below. In the silence and the heat and the glare we gazed upon a seared wasteland, a sinister and savage desolation. And found it infinitely fascinating.

We stared for a long time at the primitive little road tapering off into the nothingness of the southwest, toward fabled names on the map—Mexican Hat, Monument Valley, Navajo Mountain— and longed to follow. But we didn't. We told ourselves that we couldn't: that the old Chev would never make it, that we didn't have enough water or food or spare parts, that the radiator would rupture, the gas tank split, the retreads unravel, the water pump fail, the wheels sink in the sand—fifty good reasons—long before we ever reached civilization on the other side. Which at that time would have been about Cameron, maybe, on U.S. 89. So we turned around and slunk back to Albuquerque the way we'd come, via the pavement through Monticello, Cortez and Farmington, like common tourists.

Later, though, I acquired a pickup truck—first of a series—and became much bolder. Almost every weekend or whenever there was enough money for gas we took off, all over New Mexico, over into Arizona, up into Colorado and eventually, inevitably, back toward the Four Corners and beyond—toward whatever lay back of that beyond.

The words seem too romantic now, now that I have seen what men and heavy equipment can do to even the most angular and singular of earthly landscapes. But they suited our mood of that time. We were desert mystics, my few friends and I, the kind who read maps as others read their holy books. I once sat on the rim of a mesa above the Rio Grande for three days and nights, trying to have a vision. I got hungry and saw God in the form of a beef pie. There were other rewards. Anything small and insignificant on the map drew us with irresistible magnetism. Especially if it had a name like Dead Horse Point or Wolf Hole or Recapture

Canyon or Black Box or Old Paria (abandoned) or Hole-in-the-Rock or Paradox or Cahone (pinto bean capital of the world) or Mollie's Nipple or Dirty Devil or Pucker Pass or Pete's Mesa. Or Dandy Crossing.

Why Dandy Crossing? Obvious: because it was a dandy place to cross the river. So, one day in July 1953 we loaded the tow chain and the spare spare, the water cans and gas cans, the bedrolls and bacon and beans and boots into the back of the truck and bolted off. For the unknown. Well, unknown to us.

Discovered that, also unbeknownst to us, the pavement had been surreptitiously extended from Monticello down to Blanding while we weren't looking, some twenty miles of irrelevant tar and gravel. A trifling matter? Perhaps. But I felt even then (thirty years ago) a shudder of alarm. Something alien was moving in, something queer and out of place in the desert.

At Blanding we left the pavement and turned west on a dirt track into the sweet wilderness. Wilderness? It seemed like wilderness to us. Till we reached the town of Green River 180 miles beyond, we would not see another telephone pole. Behind us now was the last drugstore, the final power line, the ultimate policeman, the end of all asphalt, the very tip of the monster's tentacle.

We drove through several miles of pygmy forest—pinyon pine and juniper—and down into Cottonwood Wash, past Zeke's Hole and onward to the crest of Comb Ridge. Again we stopped to survey the scene. But no turning back this time. While two of my friends walked down the steep and twisting road to remove rocks and fill in holes, I followed with the pickup in compound low, riding the brake pedal. Cliff on one side, the usual thousand-foot drop on the other. I held the wheel firmly in both hands and stared out the window at my side, admiring the scenery. My girl friend watched the road.

The valley of Comb Wash looked like a form of paradise to me. There was a little stream running through the bright sand, a grove of cottonwoods, patches of grass, the color-banded cliffs on either side, the woods above—and not a house in sight, not even a cow or horse. Eden at the dawn of creation. What joy it was to know that such places still existed, waiting for us when the need arose.

We ate lunch by the stream, under the cottonwood trees, attended by a few buzzing flies and the songs of canyon wren and pinyon jay. Midsummer: the cattle were presumably all up in the mountains now, fattening on larkspur and lupine and purple penstemon. God bless them—the flowers, I mean. The wine passed back and forth among the four of us, the birds called now and then, the thin clear stream gurgled over the pebbles, bound for the San Juan River (which it would not reach, of course; sand and evaporation would see to that). Above our heads an umbrella of living, lucent green sheltered us from the July sun. We enjoyed the shade as much as the wine, the birds and flies and one another.

For another twenty miles we drove on through the pinyon-juniper woods, across the high mesa south of the Abajo Mountains. The road was rough, full of ruts and rocks and potholes, and we had to stop a few times, get out the shovel and do a little roadwork, but this was more a pleasure than otherwise. Each such stop gave all hands a chance to stretch, breathe deep, ramble, look—and see. Why hurry? It made no difference to us where nightfall might catch us. We were ready and willing to make camp anywhere. And in this splendid country, still untouched by development and industrialism, almost any spot would have made a good campsite.

Storm clouds overhead? Good. What's July in the desert without a cloudburst? My old truck creaked and rattled on. Bouncing too fast down into a deep wash I hit a pointed rock embedded in the road and punched a hole through one of the tires. We installed one of the spares and rumbled on.

Late in the afternoon we reached Natural Bridges. We drove down a steep, narrow, winding dirt lane among the pinyon

pines—fragrant with oozing gum—and into the little campground. One other car was already there. In other words, the
place was badly overcrowded, but we stayed. We spent the next
day in a leisurely triangular walk among the three great bridges—
Owachomo, Sipapu and Kachina—and a second night at the little
Park Service campground. It was the kind of campground known
as "primitive," meaning no asphalt driveways, no flush toilets, no
electric lights, no numbered campsites, no cement tables, no police patrol, no fire alarms, no traffic controls, no movies, slide
shows or press-a-button automatic tape-recorded natural history
lectures. A terrible, grim, deprived kind of campground, some
might think. Nothing but stillness, stasis and stars all night long.

In the morning we went on, deeper into the back country, back
of beyond. The "improved" road ended at Natural Bridges; from
there to the river, forty-five miles, and from there to Hanksville,
about another forty, it would be "unimproved." Good. The more
unimproved the better, that's what we thought. We assumed, in
those innocent days, that anything good would be allowed to remain that way.

Our little road wound off to the west, following a big bench,
with the sheer cliffs of a plateau on the south and the deep, com-
plicated drainages of White Canyon on the north. Beyond White
Canyon were Woodenshoe Butte, the Bear's Ears, Elk Ridge and
more fine blank areas on the maps. Nearby were tawny grass and
buff-colored cliffs, dark-green junipers and sandstone scarps.

As we descended toward the river, the country opened up,
wide and wild, with nowhere any sign of man but the dirt trail
road before us. We liked that. Why? (*Why* is always a good question.) Why not? (Always a good answer.) But why? One must
attempt to answer the question—someone always raises it, accus-
ing us of "disliking people."

Well then, it's not from simple misanthropy. Speaking generally, for myself, I like people. Speaking particularly, I like some

people, dislike others. Like everyone else who hasn't been reduced to moronism by our commercial Boy Scout ethic, I like my
friends, dislike my enemies and regard strangers with a tolerant
indifference. But why, the questioner insists, why do people like
you pretend to love uninhabited country so much? Why this cult
of wilderness? Why the surly hatred of progress and development, the churlish resistance to all popular improvements?

Very well, a fair question, but it's been asked and answered a
thousand times already; enough books to drive a man stark naked
mad have dealt in detail with the question. There are many answers, all good, each sufficient. Peace is often mentioned; beauty;
spiritual refreshment, whatever that means; re-creation for the
soul, whatever that is; escape; novelty, the delight of something
different; truth and understanding and wisdom—commendable
virtues in any man, anytime; ecology and all that, meaning the
salvation of variety, diversity, possibility and potentiality, the preservation of the genetic reservoir, the answers to questions that
we have not yet even learned to ask, a connection to the origin of
things, an opening into the future, a source of sanity for the present—all true, all wonderful, all more than enough to answer such
a dumb dead degrading question as "Why wilderness?"

To which, nevertheless, I shall append one further answer anyway: *because we like the taste of freedom; because we like the
smell of danger.*

Descending toward the river the junipers become scarce, give
way to scrubby, bristling little vegetables like black brush, snakeweed and prickly pear. The bunch grass fades away, the cliff rose
and yucca fall behind. We topped out on a small rise and there
ahead lay the red wasteland again—red dust, red sand, the dark
smoldering purple reds of ancient rocks, Chinle, Shinarump and
Moenkopi, the old Triassic formations full of radium, dinosaurs,
petrified wood, arsenic and selenium, fatal evil monstrous things,
beautiful, beautiful. Miles of it, leagues of it, glittering under the

radiant light, swimming beneath waves of heat, a great vast aching vacancy of pure space, waiting. Waiting for what? Why, waiting for us.

Beyond the red desert was the shadowy crevasse where the river ran, the living heart of the canyonlands, the red Colorado. Note my use of the past tense here. That crevasse was Glen Canyon. On either side of the canyon we saw the humps and hummocks of Navajo sandstone, pale yellow, and beyond that, vivid in the morning light, rich in detail and blue in profile, the Henry Mountains, last-discovered (or at least the last-named) mountain range within the coterminous United States. These mountains were identified, as one might expect, by Major John Wesley Powell, and named in honor of his contemporary, Joseph Henry, secretary of the Smithsonian Institution. Beyond the mountains we could see the high Thousand Lake and Aquarius plateaus, some fifty miles away by line of sight. In those days before the potash mills, cement plants, uranium mills and power plants, fifty miles of clear air was nothing—to see mountains one hundred miles away was considered commonplace, a standard of vision.

We dropped down into that red desert. In low gear. Moved cautiously across a little wooden bridge that looked as if it might have been built by old Cass Hite himself, or even Padre Escalante, centuries before. Old yellow-pine beams full of cracks and scorpions, coated with the auburn dust. Beneath the bridge ran a slit in the sandstone, a slit about ten feet wide and one hundred feet deep, so dark down in there we could hardly make out the bottom. We paused for a while to drop rocks. The sunlight was dazzling, the heat terrific, the arid air exhilarating.

I added water to the radiator, which leaked a little, as all my radiators did in my student days, and pumped up one of the tires, which had a slow leak, also to be expected, and checked the gas tank, which was a new one and did not leak, yet, although I could see dents where some rocks had got to it. We climbed aboard and went on. Mighty cumuli-nimbi massed overhead—battleships of vapor, loaded with lightning. They didn't trouble us.

We jounced along in my overloaded pickup, picking our way at two miles an hour in and out of the little ditches—deadly axle busters—that ran across, not beside the road, heading the side canyons, climbing the benches, bulling our way through the sand of the washes. We were down in the land of standing rock, the world of sculptured sandstone, crazy country, a bad dream to any dirt farmer—except for the canyon bottoms not a tree in sight.

We came to the crossing of White Canyon, where I gunned the motor hard, geared down into second, and charged through the deep sand. Old cottonwoods with elephantine trunks and sweet green trembling leaves caught my eye. Lovely things, I thought, as we crashed over a drop-off into a stream. Glimpsed sandpipers or killdeer scampering out of the way as a splash of muddy water drenched the windshield. "Hang on," I said. Heard a yelp as my friend's girl friend fell off the back of the truck. Couldn't be helped. The truck lurched up the farther bank, streaming with water, and came to halt on the level road above, more or less by its own volition.

We got out to investigate. Nobody hurt. We ate our lunch beneath the shade of the trees. In the desert, under the summer sun, a shade tree makes the difference between intolerable heat and a pleasant coolness. The temperature drops thirty degrees inside the shadow line when there is free ventilation. If homes and public buildings in the Southwest were properly designed, built for human pleasure instead of private profit, there would be no need for air conditioning. The humblest Papago peasant or Navajo sheepherder knows more about efficient hot-country architecture than a whole skyscraper full of Del Webbs.

After the siesta, in midafternoon, we drove up from the ford and around a bench of naked rock several miles long and through a notch or dugway in a red wall. Below us lay Hite, Dandy Crossing, the river.

We descended, passed a spring and more cottonwoods, and came to the combination store, gas station and post office, which was not only the business center but almost the whole of Hite. At that time I believe there were no more than three families living in the place, which must have been one of the most remote and isolated settlements in the forty-eight states. There were also a few miscellaneous individuals—prospectors, exiles, remittance men—hanging about. The total population fluctuated from year to year with the fortunes of the uranium industry. Eventually the dam was built, the river backed up and everybody flooded out.

We stopped to buy gas—fifty cents a gallon, cheap at the price—and a round of beer. I met Mr. Woody Edgell, proprietor, who was already unhappy about the future prospects of Glen Canyon. He took a dim view both of the dam and of the Utah State Highway Department's proposed bridge-building schemes for the vicinity. Not because they would put him out of the business—they wouldn't; he could relocate—but because he liked Hite and Glen Canyon the way they were, neolithic.

Not everybody felt that way. I talked with a miner's wife, and she said that she hated the place, claimed that her husband did too, and said that only lack of money kept them there. She looked forward with gratitude to the flooding of Hite—a hundred feet under water was not deep enough, she thought. She'd be glad to be forced to leave.

There was a middle-aged fellow sitting outside the store, on a bench in the shade, drinking beer. He had about a month's growth of whiskers on what passed for a face. I bought him another can of Coors and tried to draw him into conversation. He was taciturn. Would not reveal his name. When I asked him what he did around there he looked up at the clouds and over at the river and down at the ground between his boots, thinking hard, and finally said: "Nothing."

A good and sufficient answer. Taking the hint, I went away from there, leaving him in peace. My own ambition, my deepest and truest ambition, is to find within myself someday, somehow, the ability to do likewise, to do nothing—and find it enough.

Somewhat later, half waterlogged with watery beer, we went for a swim in an eddy of the river, naked, and spouted silty water at the sky. The river tugged at our bodies with a gentle but insistent urge:

Come with me, the river said, *close your eyes and quiet your limbs and float with me into the wonder and mystery of the canyons, see the unknown and the little known, look upon the stone gods face to face, see Medusa, drink my waters, hear my song, feel my power, come along and drift with me toward the distant, ultimate and legendary sea. . . .*

Sweet and subtle song. Perhaps I should have surrendered. I almost did. But didn't. We piled ourselves wet and cooled back into the truck and drove down the shore to the ferry crossing, a mile beyond the store. There was a dirt-covered rock landing built out from shore, not far, and a pair of heavy cables strung across the river to the western bank. The ferry itself was on the far side where Art Chaffin, the ferryman, lived in a big house concealed by cottonwoods. We rang the bell, as instructed by a signboard. Nothing happened. We rang it again. After a while a man appeared among the trees on the opposite shore, stepped aboard his ferry and started the engine, engaged the winch. The strange craft moved across the river's flow toward us, pulling itself along the sagging cable. It was not a boat. It appeared to be a homemade barge, a handmade contraption of wood and steel and baling wire—gasoline engine, passenger platform, vehicle ramp and railings mounted on a steel pontoon. Whatever it was, it worked, came snug against the landing. I drove my pickup aboard, we shook hands with Art Chaffin and off we went, across the golden Colorado toward that undiscovered West on the other side.

The Hite Ferry had a history, short but rich. Following old Indian trails, Cass Hite came to and named Dandy Crossing in 1883. It was one of the very few possible fords of the river in the 240 miles between Moab and Lee's Ferry. That is, it could be negotiated by team and wagon during low water (late summer, winter). But it did not become a motor vehicle crossing until 1946, when Chaffin built his ferry. The first ferry sank in 1947; Chaffin built a second, which he sold in 1956 to a man named Reed Maxfield. In 1957 Reed Maxfield had an accident and drowned in the river. His widow kept the ferry in operation until a storm in November of 1957 tore the barge loose from its mooring and sank it. By this time the ferry had become well known and its service was in some demand; the Utah State Highway Department was obliged to rebuild it. Mrs. Maxfield was hired to continue running it, which she did until Woody Edgell took over in 1959. He was the last ferryman, being finally flooded out by the impounded waters of Glen Canyon Dam in June 1964. To replace the ferry the Utah Highway Department had to build not one but three bridges: one over the mouth of the Dirty Devil, one over the Colorado at Narrow Canyon and the third over White Canyon. Because of the character of the terrain in there—hard to believe unless you see it for yourself—there is no other feasible way to get automobiles across the canyons. Thus, three big bridges, built at the cost of many million dollars, were required to perform the same service that Art Chaffin's home-designed ferry had provided adequately for eighteen years.

Back to 1953: As we were leaving the river, Mr. Chaffin, glancing at the clouded sky, advised me to watch for flash floods in North Wash.

"North Wash?" I said. "Where's that?"

"Where you're going," he said. "The only road out of here."

We followed the right bank of the river for a couple of miles upstream, rough red cliffs shutting off the view of the mountains and high country beyond. The sky was dark. The willows on the banks were lashing back and forth under a brisk wind, and a few raindrops exploded against the windshield.

Somebody suggested camping for the night beside the river, waiting out the storm. A good idea. But there was one idiot in our party who was actually *hoping* to see a flash flood. And he prevailed. In the late afternoon, under a turbulent sky, we turned away from the river and drove into a deep, narrow canyon leading west and north, where the road (you might call it that) wound up and out, toward the open country twenty miles above. According to my road map. Which also said, quote, *Make local inquiry before attempting travel in this area.*

A good canyon. A little creek came down it, meandering between vertical walls. The road crossed that stream about ten times per mile, out of necessity. I tested the brakes occasionally. Wet drums. No brakes. But it hardly mattered, since we were ascending. The sprinkling of rain had stopped, and everyone admired the towering canyon walls, the alcoves and grottoes, the mighty boulders strewn about on the canyon floor. The air was cool and sweet, the tamarisk and redbud and box elders shivered in the breeze on their alluvial benches. Flowers bloomed, as I recall. Birds chirruped now and then, humble and discreet.

I became aware of a deflating tire and stopped the pickup in the middle of the wash, spanning the rivulet of clear water. It was the only level place immediately available.

Our girl friends walked ahead up the road while my buddy and I jacked up the truck and pulled the wheel. We checked the tire and found that we'd picked up a nail, probably by the Hite store.

We were standing there bemused and barefooted, in the stream, when we heard the women begin to holler from somewhere out of sight up the canyon. Against the noise of the wind, and something like a distant waterfall, it was hard to make out their words.

Mud? Blood? Flood?

As we stood there discussing the matter I felt a sudden surge in the flow of water between my ankles. Looking down, I saw that the clear water had turned into a thick, reddish liquid, like tomato soup.

Our spare tire was packed away beneath a load of duffle, pots and pans and grub boxes. So we jammed the flat tire back on and lugged it down quick with a couple of nuts. My friend picked up the hub cap before it floated away with the rest of the wheel nuts, and stared up the canyon. We couldn't see anything yet but we could hear it—a freight train rolling full speed down North Wash. Where there never was a railway.

We jumped in the truck, I started the motor and tried to drive away. The engine roared but nothing moved. One wheel still jacked off the ground. No positive traction in that pickup. We had to get out again; we pushed the truck forward, off the jack, and discovered that it was in gear. The truck humped ahead and stalled. The main body of the flood appeared around the bend up canyon. We got back in the truck and lurched and yawed, flat tire flopping, out of the bottom of the wash and onto the safety of higher ground. The flood roared past below.

The girls joined us. There was no rain where we stood, and the ground was dry. But we could feel it tremble. From within the flood, under the rolling red waters, we heard the grating of rocks as they clashed on one another, a sound like the grinding of molars in leviathan jaws.

Our road was cut off ahead and behind. We camped on the bench that evening, made supper in the violet twilight of the canyon while thousands of cubic tons of semiliquid sand, silt, mud, rock, uprooted junipers, logs, a dead cow, rumbled by twenty feet away.

The juniper fire smelled good. The food was even better. A few clear stars switched on in that narrow slot of sky between the canyon walls overhead. We built up the fire and sang. My girl friend was beautiful. My friend's girl friend was beautiful. My old pickup truck was beautiful, and life itself seemed like a pretty good deal.

Sometime during the night the flood dropped off and melted away, almost as abruptly as it had come. We awoke in the morning to the music of canyon wrens and a trickling stream, and found that our road was still in the canyon, though kind of folded over and tucked in and rolled up in corners here and there. It took us considerable roadwork and all day long to get out of North Wash. And it was worth every minute of it. Never had such interesting work again till the day I tried to take a Hertz rental Super-Sport past Squaw Spring and up Elephant Hill in The Needles. Or the time another friend and I carried his VW Beetle down through Pucker Pass off Dead Horse Point after a good rain.

At North Wash we had a midday rest at Hog Spring, halfway out. We met a prospector in a jeep coming in. He said we'd never make it. Hogwash. We said he'd never make it. He looked as pleased as we were, and went on.

Today the old North Wash trail road is partly submerged by the reservoir, the rest obliterated. The state has ripped and blasted and laid an asphalt highway through and around the area to link the new tin bridges with the outside world. The river is gone, the ferry is gone, Dandy Crossing is gone. Most of the formerly primitive road from Blanding west has been improved beyond recognition. All of this, the engineers and politicians and bankers will tell you, makes the region easily accessible to everybody, no matter how fat, feeble or flaccid. That is a lie.

It is a lie. For those who go there now, smooth, comfortable, quick and easy, sliding through as slick as grease, will never be able to see what we saw. They will never feel what we felt. They will never know what we knew, or understand what we cannot forget.

THREE

DAYS AND NIGHTS
IN OLD PARIAH

 The local Utah cowboys (they number about a dozen souls, all living in Kanab or, during working hours, in the Buckskin Tavern just across the Arizona line) call it the Pyorrhea. The Utes called it Pah, meaning "water," and Reah, meaning "dirty." Pah-reah, "dirty water." The early Spanish explorers españolized the name to Paria. I like Pariah.

I'm talking about a canyon, an abandoned Mormon village, and a small perennial stream that begins near Bryce

Canyon National Park and empties itself eighty-five meandering, malingering, maligned miles later into what's left of the Colorado River at Lee's Ferry.

I haven't seen it all. I wonder if anyone has. But I've seen a great deal of it, together with Buckskin Gulch, a major tributary, and it is one of my favorite secret places in the canyon country.

Old Pariah is on the maps. You turn north off the highway onto a nice ill-graded, maybe never-graded and always treacherous dirt road, which takes you after a few miles down among the lung-colored, liver-hued bentonite hills of the Pariah Valley.

The first thing you will see is a fake ghost town, made of secondhand lumber, built by Hollywood a few years ago for some mediocre movie. Nobody lives here. Nobody ever did. A single dirt street leads between two rows of false fronts—saloon, hotel, livery stable, jail—all phony as Disneyland. Some of the houses appear to rest on rock footing, but check them close and you find chicken wire and plaster. The buildings have no walls in the rear; they were built that way to allow easy access for cameras and booms. From certain angles Hollywood Pariah looks like a half-dismantled mining camp.

The boards creak and crack under the pitiless sun. When the wind blows, which is most of the time, you hear its melancholy moan through the empty wooden shells, the rattle of loose roofing, the rustle of tumbleweeds and tin cans, the swirl of red dust down the abandoned street. At midnight the town becomes still as starlight. Under the moon it appears as an intricate diagram of pale surfaces, rusted roofs, inky angles, black and impenetrable shadows.

If other tourists ever find this place, it seems likely that most will mistake the Hollywood construct for the real Pariah. But the real Pariah is different.

You follow the dirt track for another mile beyond the fake ghost town till you come to the silt and sand bottoms of the Pariah

River. Unless the ground is frozen it is best to park your vehicle and walk; even a four-wheel-drive truck can get bogged down in the muck beyond. You wade across the river, which, except when in flood, is no more than ankle deep, and climb the left, or eastern, bank. Here, scattered over a mile of rocky benchland, some of it shaded by cottonwoods, are the ruins of the original town.

There are not many. Founded in 1874, Pariah never had a population greater than a hundred humans. The Mormon settlers attempted to farm the bottomlands along the stream, but the frequent floods, the alkaline soil and the mineralized water made agriculture a hopeless project. In 1890 the town was deserted, and no one has tried to make a permanent habitation of it since. Only the cattle, property of a Kanab rancher, make any use of the shade and shelter provided by the old cabins, expertly constructed of sandstone slabs hauled from the nearby cliffs. Some of the stone lintels over the doors and windows are five feet long, four inches thick. On most are the ripple marks left by the waves of an ancient sea.

So here at Pariah we have two ghost towns, one real, one false; one of stone, one of wood; one recent, the other over a century old; both in ruin, both sad and strange, both forgotten in a setting of surrealistic rock, malevolent and glowing color—a radiant wasteland.

Buckskin Gulch is the Pariah's major tributary. The Gulch is almost as long as the Pariah itself, commencing beneath the pink cliffs of the Paunsaugunt and leading nearly to the Arizona line, where it enters Pariah Canyon at grade level, eight hundred feet below rimrock. The last six or seven miles of Buckskin Gulch are said to be fantastically deep and narrow—"so deep and narrow," one Kanab old-timer told me, "you can see the stars in the daytime"—and it was of course this portion we hoped to see.

We began our hike—John De Puy, Judy Colella and I—off the dirt road in Houserock Valley, following the gulch that we guessed was Buckskin toward the east, into a Byzantine region of sandstone domes, turrets, pinnacles, minarets, alcoves, grottoes and amphitheaters.

August: the sand was damp and firm, having recently been flooded. Pools of stagnant water stood in the shade of boulders and mud banks, perceptibly evaporating—we could feel the humidity. A few clouds drifted overhead. We passed through something like a portal, a gateway in the rock, entering a hidden basin of sand, rice grass, juniper and tumbleweed enclosed within a giant bowl of almost totally nude, monolithic sandstone hundreds of feet high. A weird place, silent as the moon.

Just before the entrance to the narrows we found a heifer embedded to her belly in wet quicksand. Judging from the amount of dung beneath her tail the poor beast may have been trapped there for twenty-four hours. She'd given up struggling, anyway, though she was still alive. We tried to get her out but failed, the gelatinous sand flowing back as fast as we could remove it with our hands. Rather than struggle there all day we decided to go on, thinking that the heifer would be able to extricate herself by her own efforts as the quicksand dried out. We expected to return by the same way.

We entered a second portal in the rock and found ourselves in a deep and narrow gulch. The walls on either side were sheer sandstone, unscalable. As we tramped deeper into this natural corridor we looked ahead, at each turning of the way, for an exit, an escape route up and out. None in sight. It must have occurred to John and Judy as well as me that it was a foolhardy thing to go into such a place in the middle of the rainy season. A cloudburst could have filled the upper reaches of the Buckskin miles away without our having any notion of it; a nice fat flash flood might already be rolling down upon us from the rear. But none of us mentioned the possibility. Perhaps from fear of reinforcing fear. We slogged on, into the shadows, into the muck, into the abyss. Fortunately for fools there was no storm that day.

The pools of water got deeper, the quicksand sloppier the farther we went. We could wade the former, but it became increasingly harder to slide and skate over the surface of the latter. Whenever we paused to inspect the descent beyond we discovered our feet sinking; several times whole banks and shelves of the stuff would start to move beneath us and slough off into the water.

We were about to give up when John spotted sunlight ahead. An opening. We plowed through the last hundred yards of glue, under overhanging walls four or five hundred feet high, and out into a wide place in the canyon with sunshine, elbowroom, a pocket of life.

We sat down to dry out, poured the silt out of our boots, ate some lunch. Petroglyphs on the clean-cut walls: we inspected them. And a winding slit off to the right—a possible exit? We'd investigate that later. Lacking a map, we had only the dimmest idea how far we were from the main canyon of the Pariah. Five miles? Ten miles? We proceeded.

The walls closed in again. We tramped down a rocky hallway five feet wide and five hundred feet deep. Above us the walls were so near one another in places, and so angled, that we could not see the sky. Nor any stars. Wedged crosswise between the walls, sometimes twenty feet above our heads, were logs—driftwood left behind by a flood. High-water marks. Some looked as if the weight of a bird might dislodge them.

The gravel, pebbles and rocks disappeared beneath new layers of muck. We sank in to our thighs. Around another bend we saw long pools of muddy water waiting for us, and more shores of quicksand, and the subterranean passage winding on and on into twilight, deeper and deeper through the plateau. By now it was late in the afternoon.

We agreed to return. Heaving ourselves through the mud back to firm terrain, we explored the side slit and found that it would go up and out of the canyon.

On the surface of the world again, baking happily in the August heat, we looked around for Buckskin Gulch. We stood on the rolling and canted surface of the Pariah Plateau, a maze of naked sandstone domes. Dark cracks were visible here and there: any one of them might be a canyon hundreds of feet deep.

We tramped around over the hills and through the dunes, found flowers and yucca and juniper and an old Anasazi chipping ground, startled a bunch of half-wild cattle, took a dip in a sandy pothole and started back. We did not descend into the canyon again; instead we followed its winding rim.

When John and Judy stopped in a shady place to draw pictures in their sketchbooks, I refilled my canteen and climbed a sloping scarp. On top, among knolls and reefs and capitol domes of totally nude stone (I mean not a single weed, not even a blade of grass), I found a group of potholes. There must have been thirty within an area of ten acres, all filled with water from the recent rains. I went swimming in one that was about 150 feet in diameter and seven feet deep at the center.

Wriggling about in the water with me were swarms of tadpoles, mosquito larvae, a variety of water beetle known locally as "boatman" and the fantastic fairy shrimp, *Apus acquelius*, which looks like a miniature horseshoe crab—or trilobite. A type of freshwater crustacean, it probably is a direct descendant of the Paleozoic trilobite, which it so closely resembles. An eerie feeling, to contemplate at six-inch range this helmet-headed grope-thing with its eyeless brow, serried ranks of villuslike feet and long, forked, jointed tail—like facing the primeval here and now. I thought of the ancient slime from which we came; I thought of our earth as it will be one billion sun-years hence, when such things as these may be all the life that remains.

A sensational storm was brewing in the southwestern skies: streamers of wind-whipped cloud, lined with lightning, flew before the sun. *(Oh black and scarlet banners of revolt! of hope! of free beer!*) I slid and scurried down the sculptured mounds of sandstone to my friends and the patient heifer.

Yes, on our return we found her still in place, cemented in the dried and hardened sand. There went the evening. We spent two hours digging that brute out with hands and sticks. Freeing one hoof was not sufficient. We had to excavate all four, and even then, apparently exhausted, she could not rise from the four holes in which our labor left her standing. I found a cedar fence post and with that we levered her out of the ground. Out of the grave. She still wanted to die. We grabbed her by the tail and hoisted her rear, then the head. She trembled, took a few wobbly steps like a newborn calf, halted and looked back at us. Grateful? Not that we could notice. I gave her a gentle boot in the hinder end to liven up her spirits. She shambled off, headed for grass and water. We went our ways.

The storm, which had looked so promising, blew away that evening but returned two days later in full Augustan glory. I presume that Buckskin Gulch was filled, flushed and scoured once again. I hope our heifer got out of there in time.

Six weeks later I was back on the old Pariah, determined this time to go all the way. With me was Tom Lyon of Logan, wearing sandals. (He carried a pair of canvas sneakers in his pack.) Starting from near the highway where the Pariah cuts through the Cockscomb, we walked for three and a half days and came out at Lee's Ferry. We celebrated with a swim in the icy green Colorado River.

Along the way—forty miles—we saw nothing but cavernous gorges; quicksand; high sheer tapestried walls of golden sandstone; marvelous patterns of light and shade on rock; water and cottonwood trees, green cottonwoods beginning to turn to gold; the boggy impassable mouth of Buckskin Gulch; freshwater seeps and springs; hanging gardens on the canyon walls; side canyons; an abandoned river channel; waterfalls and plunge pools, potsherds and petroglyphs; remains of a pump station where Mormon ranchers back in the 1920s had tried to raise water from the stream to the plateau one thousand feet above; a two-hundred-foot natural arch; a deserted homestead; old cowboy trails; signs of deer, coyote and bighorn sheep; immense sand dunes; blazing meteors by night and a radiant sun by day; and for the last ten miles an extensive panorama of plateau escarpments, sand mountains, the Echo Cliffs and the original sky. Routine stuff.

Tom's sandals gave out about halfway. It was a noble experiment. My back ached from carrying twenty pounds too much dehydrated enchiladas and freeze-dried bouillabaisse, an ignoble experiment; the trouble was we walked too fast and didn't eat enough. We should have spent ten days on that trip. I believe I'd be willing to spend 10 percent of the rest of my life in the canyons of Pariah—if they leave them alone. Twenty percent if they let me alone.

Luckily for those who prefer their canyons natural, it seems unlikely that Pariah will ever be subjected to official improvement or motorized invasion. Vertical walls, the narrow canyon floor, frequent and vigorous floods, make any kind of road unfeasible. Because of soft sand, spongy gravel, boulder jams and the lengthy stretches of quicksand, anyone who tries to get through here on a trail bike or similar frivolous device will find himself toting his bike on his back for most of the forty miles; even a saddle horse would be a tough proposition. The Bureau of Land Management plans to install "a few discreet signs" within the canyon to indicate points of interest, but these will be removed by the first flood to come along—or by the first thoughtful hiker. Initiative and enterprise, that's what made America great.

FOUR

DESERT IMAGES

Of all natural forms the sand dunes are the most elegant—so simple, severe, bare. Nature in the nude. Nothing can mar for long their physical integrity. Broken down by foot traffic or machines, the sand is re-formed by the winds into fresh new dunes, formally perfect, advancing with the winds across the desert, where nothing but a mountain range can halt their progress.

Sand—unlike dust—is not airborne at great altitudes. Students of the matter have learned that even the strongest winds can seldom lift sand more than a foot or two above the ground. Where the ground is hard and fairly flat, however, the wind steady, the supply of sand sufficient, this lifting power is enough to form dunes.

A dune begins with any obstacle on the surface—a stone, a shrub, a log, anything heavy enough to resist being moved by the wind. This obstacle forms a *wind shadow* on its leeward side, resulting in eddies in the current of the air, exactly as a rock in a stream causes an eddy in the water. Within the eddy the wind moves with less force and velocity than the airstreams on either side, creating what geologists call *the surface of discontinuity*. Here the wind tends to drop part of its load of sand. The sand particles, which should be visualized as hopping or bouncing along the surface before the wind (not flying through the air), begin to accumulate, the pile grows higher, becoming itself a barrier to the wind, creating a greater eddy in the air currents and capturing still more sand. The formation of a dune is under way.

Viewed in cross section, sand dunes display a characteristic profile. On the windward side the angle of ascent is low and gradual—twenty to twenty-five degrees from the horizontal. On the leeward side the slope is much steeper, usually about thirty-four degrees—the angle of repose of sand and most other loose materials. The steep side of the dune is called the *slip face* because of the slides that take place as sand is driven up the windward side and deposited on and just over the crest. When the deposit on the crest becomes greater than can be supported by the sand beneath, the extra sand slumps down the slip face. As the process is repeated through the years, the whole dune advances with the direction of the prevailing wind, until some obstacle like a mountain intervenes. At this point the dunes, prevented from advancing, pile higher. At Death Valley and in Great Sand Dunes National Monument in Colorado the highest dunes reach five hundred feet. The only higher sand dunes are in Iran, where they attain a world's record of seven hundred feet.

Seen from the bird's point of view, most of these desert sand dunes have a crescent shape, like the new moon. The horns of the crescent point downwind, with the slip face on the inside of the curve. This type of dune is called a *barchan*—a Russian term. (A sea of sand, as in Mexico's Gran Desierto near the mouth of the Colorado River, is called an *erg*, a Hamitic word.) Dunes sometimes take other forms. There are transverse dunes, ridges of sand lying at a right angle to the course of the wind, and longitudinal dunes, which lie parallel to the wind. And there are parabolic dunes—barchans in reverse. Why dunes assume these different shapes is a question not yet resolved by those who have studied the problem.

How fast does a sand dune move? About twenty-five feet, sometimes up to fifty feet, in a year. Eventually the dunes achieve a point where they can advance no farther, climb no higher. When this happens, they resume the equally ancient process of consolidating themselves into sandstone. Into rock. We are talking here of a leisurely natural process, of millions of years. Sand and rock may observe a cosmic timetable, may follow some kind of pulse of their own, but if so this lies beyond human comprehension.

In our traditional conception of the desert we imagine it consisting entirely of billowing seas of sand, with here and there a palm tree, a gaunt saguaro cactus, the skull of a cow emerging from the sandy waves. Not so. Most of the Great American Desert is made up of bare rock, rugged cliffs, mesas, canyons, mountains, separated from one another by broad flat basins covered with sun-baked mud and alkali, supporting a sparse and measured growth of sagebrush or creosote or saltbush, depending on location and elevation. In the American desert sand dunes are rather rare, relative to the size of the area of which they are a part. Death Valley; the San Luis Valley in Colorado; Monument Valley in Arizona and Utah; the White Sands of New Mexico; the sand dunes near Yuma, Arizona, and in the Mojave Desert of Southern California; a few places in Nevada—that sums it up. But like many things that are rare, a field of dunes makes up in beauty what it lacks in vast expanse.

A simple but always varied beauty. Shades of color that change from hour to hour—bright golden in morning and afternoon, a pallid tan beneath the noon sun, platinum by moonlight, blue-sheened under snow, metallic silver when rimed with hoarfrost, glowing like heated iron at sunrise and sunset, lavender by twilight. With forms and volumes and masses inconstant as wind but always shapely. Dunes like nude bodies. Dunes like standing waves. Dunes like arcs and sickles, scythe blades and waning moons. Virgin dunes untracked by machines, untouched by human feet. Dunes firm and solid after rain, ribbed with ripple marks from the wind. Dunes surrounding ephemeral pools of water that glitter golden as tiger's eye in the light of dawn. The clear-cut cornice of a dune, seen from below, carving out of the intense blue of the sky a brazen, brassy arc of monumental particulars. Yes—and the dunes that flow around and upon a dying mesquite tree in the Mojave, suffocating a stand of junipers and yellow pine in some lovely piece of back-country Utah. Sand and beauty. Sand and death. Sand and renewal.

It is time for a walk on the dunes. There may not be many years left. I leave the road and walk out on the dunes, following the delicate footprints of a fox. Past the arrowweed on the salt flats, past the little bosks of mesquite in the foothills of the dunes, up the windward side along the crest where the sand is so firm my feet leave only a faint impression. On the sand are other tracks even more delicate than those of the fox—the imprints of mice, beetles, lizards, birds.

I trail my fox into the lifeless heart of Death Valley, wondering where he might be bound. The morning sun rises higher above the purple Grapevine Mountains on the east, illuminates with a rosy glow the Panamint Mountains on the west. The tracks go high, then descend, then climb still higher on the next and greater dune. In general, with all its wandering, the fox seems to be bearing toward the highest dune of them all, four hundred feet above the valley floor. That fox should be hungry; a fox in the wild lives mostly on the keen edge of starvation. Yet his course is leading him farther and farther from any likely source of food. The fox's prey live below, among the clumps of vegetation between the dunes; the tracks of rodents and lizards become scarce, then nonexistent, as we climb higher.

Maybe this fox is crazy. Or rabid. Or old and looking for a place to die. Or a sightseer like me. Why the summit of the sands? Yet that is where the trail finally leads me. To the high point of the highest dune. And there, as I can plainly read on the open page of the sand, the fox paused for a while, turning in one place, before plunging over the cornice and down, in great leaps, through the soft, unstable sand of the slip face, disappearing into the brush on the flats below.

What brought that fox up here? I don't know. A light wind is blowing now and all tracks, including my own, are beginning to soften, blur, fade out in a serried pattern of ripples in the sand. I lie belly down on the cornice of the dune, looking over the edge. Fine grains of sand, backlit by the sun, shining like particles of light, are swirling in the air. I can hear them tinkling and chiming as they fall on the sand below. Like crystals of quartz; like tiny fragments of broken glass. There is no other sound in this desert world.

I roll over on my back and gaze up at the cloudless, perfect, inhuman, unsheltering sky. The inevitable vulture soars there, a thousand feet above me. Black wings against the blue. I think I know that bird. He looks familiar. I think he's the one that's been following me, everywhere I go in the desert, for about thirty-five years. Looking after me. I follow the fox. The vulture follows me.

🕊

"I love all things that flow," said James Joyce. "If there is magic on this earth it lies in water," Loren Eiseley said. And nowhere is water so beautiful as in the desert, for nowhere else is it so scarce. By definition. Water, like a human being or a tree or a bird or a song, gains value by rarity, singularity, isolation. In a humid climate, water is common. In the desert each drop is precious.

Way down in a corner of Arizona, near the Mexican border, is a tiny spring called Sweet Water. This spring is the only permanent, reliable, natural source of water between Quitobaquito on the east and the Tinajas Altas ("High Tanks") on the west—a distance of sixty miles by road. That road, surfaced in sand alternating with long stretches of blue-black lava rock, was called the Vulture's Road. Long since abandoned, bypassed by paved highways far to the north and south, the Vulture's Road can still be followed here and there, the route identifiable by dim tracks across the stone, by cast-off wagon-wheel rims and antique Ford mufflers dissolving in rust and by the mounds of stones and iron crosses that mark the burial sites of those who never made it. No one with any brains ever traveled that road in summer. In winter the low desert can be comfortable, even exhilarating, if you're properly equipped for survival; but in summer it is intolerable. The shimmer of heat waves, hanging like a scrim across the horizon, is enough in itself to confuse the senses, puzzle the mind. The mountains float like ships on the waves of superheated air, drifting away from one another, then returning, merging, inverting themselves, assuming shapes out of fantasy. The madness of mirage.

Some of those passing on that road must have wondered, as they endured the heat and the thirst, what lay within the folds of a certain small mountain range to the north. A typical desert range: blue hills prickly with cactus, agave, spiny shrubs and stinging nettles, mostly bare of any vegetation at all, scaled and plated with loose rock, the high ridges notched with points like a dragon's backbone. What a few men knew was that there was water in there—the spring of Sweet Water. Not that the knowledge would have done the travelers much good. The spring is far from the road, difficult to reach; the effort required to get there might have taken more lives than the little trickle of water could have saved. In the desert it is usually more important to ration bodily energy than water itself; sweat may be as costly as blood.

One morning in March I drove my government truck into the area, through the cactus forest to the end of the dim track, then walked the last few miles. I had plenty of water with me and within me; I was being paid to patrol these parts, investigate worked-out gold mines, check game trails, inspect animal droppings, test the water of hidden tanks and secret springs.

There is no man-made trail, only a deer path, a bighorn-sheep path, a lion run, leading to the spring. The stones are loose and tricky, the drop-offs vertical, the brush and cactus thick, resistant, hostile. One proceeds with care. A broken leg could be a serious mistake, especially when alone. Accidents are forbidden. But the birds like it here: I was serenaded on my way by the sharp whistles of a thrasher—that signal so humanlike that the first few times you hear it you always stop and look around, expecting to see a boy or another man. Or a woman, now that women have liberated themselves from certain genteel constraints. ("Whistling girls and crowing hens," my grandmother used to say, "both shall come to no good ends.")

Other birds are also present. I heard a cactus wren, its voice like the chatter of a rusty adding machine. And the sweet brief tunes of cardinal, pyrrhuloxia, phainopepla—the last a shy and furtive little bird, hard to get to know.

I reached a saddle in the mountains without finding the spring, though the convergence of tracks left by many small feet suggested that I was getting close. Plus the variety of scat on the trail: not only bighorn sheep and deer but also coyote, rabbit, kit fox and the messy little clots of dung of the javelina, the wild pig or peccary of the southwestern deserts.

Once on the other side of the saddle and around a few more overhangs of rotten volcanic rock and through a tunnel in the thorny mesquite and catclaw acacia, where I crawled on hands and knees to save the shirt from being torn off my back, I found the spring. It was easy to spot: a clump of leafless but conspicuously coppery willows, a dwarf cottonwood barely beginning to leaf out with the soft green of a new growing season. The little trees made only a patch of deciduous life in the midst of many square miles of blue stone and olive-drab desert growth, but that single tiny patch was sufficient to indicate the presence of the desert's sweetest miracle—surface water. Or at the least, water very close to the surface. About fifty yards short of the spring and a little above it, downwind from the prevailing westerlies, I came upon a blind of saguaro ribs. I squatted down in the lattice shade of the thing armed with binoculars, notebook, a canteen of water, a hunk of longhorn cheese, a box of raisins, and I waited.

The sun went down. I put on my coat as the temperature dropped ten, fifteen, twenty degrees within twenty minutes. Binoculars ready, I watched the water hole—the only water hole within twenty miles. The bird songs faded away. Crickets began to rub their fore wings together down by the spring. The lavender dusk, in a precipitation of colors too subtle to name, spread across the desert hills, through the sky, across Sonora to the south, across the fifty miles of landscape within my range of sight. The sickle of moon grew brighter.

Most desert animals do not require water daily. The deer, the bighorn sheep, the javelina are believed to go two or three days at a time without a drink, getting by, that is, on what they've stored in their tissues. Early March, also, is not the best of times for finding wildlife at a water hole; cool days, natural tanks full of winter rains, fresh plant growth make needs less pressing. Midsummer—July, August, September—that's the best time. It was quite possible, therefore, that I would see nothing.

I waited. The air grew chillier, the moon slipped lower, the night came on. One more hour, I resolved, and then I give up; then it's back up the trail by moonlight and down the other side, back to the truck, a beer, something hot to eat, before laying out my bedroll on the desert floor.

I heard the clash of stone far down in the brush-filled ravine below the spring. I raised the field glasses and studied the area but could see nothing in motion. I waited, changing position again to ease my aching limbs. Again I heard the slight, faint, far-off click of something hard on stone. An animal was approaching, and as I watched, concentrating on the mesquite and acacia thickets, I saw first one then a second sleek, gracile, dun-colored form appear, climbing on delicate hoofs up the path toward the spring. Followed by a third, a fourth, a fifth, all in single file. And then two more. And still more, at least a dozen in all, quiet as shadows, pale and obscure as the twilight, bodies barely distinguishable from the dark background of stone and brush.

For a moment I thought they were small deer. But all young bucks! With black spikes. And then I recognized them as desert pronghorn, a species almost extinct in the United States, though once quite numerous in southern Arizona. These had probably come up from Mexico, sliding under the fence like illegal immigrants. I was glad to see them. They gathered about the spring, jostling one another until the basic order of precedence was re-established, then drank, two or three at a time while the others waited and watched. I could hear the gurgling of water passing rapidly down those parched throats, the sighs and grunts of satisfaction. There is something in the feeding and drinking of large animals that gives, to the human onlooker, a sensation of deep pleasure. Mammalian empathy, perhaps.

Finally the pronghorns had enough. A long time, as it seemed to me, for of course I had to wait until the last had drunk its fill before I could stir; I didn't want to scare away from a much needed watering the lowest pronghorn in the pecking order. Not until all turned and started back the way they'd come did I stand up. At once, with a clatter of stones and armored feet, they took off. A dozen white rump patches flashed in the moonlight, vanishing two seconds later into the gloom below—soon gone beyond earshot as well as sight. I walked down and inspected the spring. A ring of dampness showed that the pronghorns had lowered the water level eight inches. I felt the muddy residue, then cupped my hands under the trickle that flowed from the algae-covered rock and drank.

Satisfied I followed the path back to the saddle of the mountain, through the moonlit tangle of cactus and brush, over the rocks, back to my headquarters for the night.

🦶

Life is gaunt and spare in the desert; that's what old time desert rats like best about it. They feel they cannot breathe properly without at least a cubic mile of unshared space about them. Let another man or woman appear on their horizon and they begin to feel the urge to decamp, move on, climb to the pass, investigate that purple range of barren hills beyond the gleaming salt flats, find out what's going on up in there, among those shadowy valleys, those ragged battlements of broken-down rock. Where, as they should know damn well, they'll find nothing but the same scatter of dried-out brittlebush, the same fireplugs of barrel cactus with spines like fishhooks, the same herd of feral burros gaping at them from the ridgeline, the same dun-colored rattler coiled beneath a limestone shelf, waiting its chance to strike. Don't tread on me.

Desert plant life is much the same—private. Even the commonest shrub, like the creosote bush, keeps its distance from the next. Each sets alone inside an ample circle of open ground. Botanists say that the roots of the plant secrete a poison, a growth inhibitor, that prevents new, seedling creosote from getting a start within that charmed circle of solitariness.

So it is with the flowers of the desert, though not without some exceptions. In certain years, not frequent, when the winter drizzles have fallen at the right times in the correct amounts, and when the weather achieves exactly the proper balance in March and April between heat and cold, sunlight and cloud cover, you may be lucky enough to see whole desert valleys and hills covered, "carpeted" as they say, with a solid blaze of flowering Mexican poppy, or globe mallow, or mimulus or coreopsis. These are splendid and rare occasions, attracting flower freaks, photographers, and desert flora fanciers from half the cities of the nation, odd people who think nothing of grabbing a jet plane and flying two thousand miles to see the flare-up of sudden orange when the *Calochortus kennedyi* takes over some Mojave valley down in California's wastelands. That or the Mexican poppies. Or the brittlebush itself, an otherwise humble and obscure knee-high shrub, which can perform wonders: nothing is more striking than to see the grim black cinder cones in the Pinacate Lava Fields take on suddenly—almost overnight—a rash of yellow, when twenty thousand brittlebushes break out in simultaneous golden bloom. Ridiculous. And sublime.

But these are, as said, the exceptions. Generally the flowers of the desert reveal themselves in solitary splendor. A primrose lurking on a sand dune. A single paloverde flaring by an arid watercourse. One woolly clump of *Baileya multiradiata* gracing the edge of the asphalt, shivering in the breeze from forty-ton freight trucks. The great *Agave palmeri*, or century plant, blooms only once in its entire existence ("the garland briefer than a girl's"), but in that supreme assertion of love and continuity it more than justifies the sacrifice required. For a decade or so the century plant grows, emerging slowly from the rock; the heavy spine-tipped blades that function as leaves wax fat, with an interlocking bulge in the center resembling an artichoke. Here the food and energy are stored. One spring a signal is given—we don't know what or why. The bulge unfolds, like a slow-motion explosion, and a shaft rises from the center, growing rapidly, reaching a height of ten or twelve feet within a week. This is the flower stalk, efflorescing as it rises with a series of alternate flower-bearing stems from midpoint to the top. The yellowish, heavy blooms wait there, upright on the towering stalk, for a week, two weeks, are pollinated by bats and insects, then begin to fade. As they fade the plant dies slowly, by degrees, from stem to root, though the strong, rigid shaft, supported by the base, may stand erect for a year after death. The death does not matter; the seeds have been sown.

The desert offers a second outburst of flowering in September and October, after the customary summer rains. This is the time of the globe mallow, or pink-eye poppy as it's also known, and rabbit brush, a stinking shrub with a showy display of yellow bloom, and the sunflowers—acres and acres of waist-high mule-ear (so named for the shape of the leaves) *Helianthus annuus*, visible from miles away.

Down in dank and shady places grows a shady customer—moonflower, angel's-trumpet, the sacred *Datura meteloides*. A large gross ivory-colored thing, set amid dark and shiny green leaves, the whole plant, flowers, stem, leaves, roots, is rich in scopolamine, a potent alkaloid much prized by witch doctors. The correct dosage is said to be spiritually rewarding, but the problem is that a microgram too much may lead to convulsions, paralysis and death—also rewarding, perhaps, but usually considered premature.

I try to think of a favorite among my arid-country flowers. But I love them all. How could we be true to one without being false to all the others? Just the same I think I'll praise a few more individuals here, single them out from among the crowd.

The cliffrose, for example. A flowering shrub, *Cowania mexicana*, a true member of the rose family, the cliffrose can be found in many parts of the mesa country and high desert from Colorado to California. The shrub may grow from four to twelve feet high. Twisted and gnarled like a juniper, it is relatively inconspicuous most of the year. But in April and May it blooms, putting out a thick, showy cluster of pale yellow or cream-colored flowers with the fragrance of orange blossoms. On a breezy day in spring you can smell the faint, delicate but heart-intoxicating sweetness for miles. The cliffrose is a bold plant, flourishing in the most improbable places, clinging to the cliff's edge, overhanging the rim of a plateau, gracing the pockets of sand far out among the slickrock domes. Deer, bighorn sheep, domestic sheep and cattle all browse on the leaves of this plant in the winter, when little else is available.

Or how about the wild morning glory, *Evolvulus arizonicus*? Another beauty. A hardy annual that blooms from April to October. The flowers are small, scarcely half an inch in diameter, but of so clear and striking an azure blue, especially in contrast to the tiny leaves and scraggly stems of the plant itself, that they assert themselves—against the sun-bleached background of sand and rock—with eye-catching vigor.

Several varieties of lupine grow in the desert. In Arizona the violet-purple *Lupinus sparsiflorus*, in western Texas the blue-purple *L. havardii*, in southwest California the royal-purple *L. odoratus*. Bushy members of the pea family, the lupines generally grow from two to three feet tall in clusters along roadways, trails, and the edges of valley bottoms, wherever the runoff from rains tends to be a little heavier. Sometimes they grow in pure stands, turning the burnt umber and dun brown of the desert into a wind-shimmering lake of blue-pink-purple radiance. The lupine is not good for anything bankable; hungry livestock eat them, get sick and die (alkaloids). All they have to offer us is their own rare beauty.

One more. A secret flower, a hidden special, little known, seldom publicized: the desert prince's plume, *Stanleya pinnata*, a man-high plant that blooms from May to July in some of the hottest, dreariest, most godforsaken and otherwise life-forsaken places in the Southwest. In dried-out mud flats along arid watercourses; on the shale and gravel talus slopes under a Moenkopi-formation rock bluff; around the alkaline edges of some desperate mudhole way out in the clay hills, the badlands, the Painted Desert. The flowers stand up in golden spikes, racemes of bright yellow blazing against the red cliffs and blue sky.

In those secret canyon glens where the hanging gardens grow, nourished on water percolating through the sandstone, you'll find yellow columbine. Certainly as beautiful a flower as anything on earth, though not so large and spectacular as the blue columbine of the mountains. Many others live here too, delicate as angel's breath, and tough. They've got to be tough, surviving in those precarious perches on a perpendicular slickrock wall.

And then you walk out in the badlands and see a single Indian paintbrush lifting its cup of salmon-colored, petallike bracts toward the sky. The paintbrush too is beautiful, with the special and extraordinary beauty of wild and lonely things. Every desert flower shares that quality. Anything that lives where it would seem that nothing could live, enduring extremes of heat and cold, sunlight and storm, parching aridity and sudden cloudbursts, among burnt rock and shifting sands, any such creature—beast, bird or flower—testifies to the grandeur and heroism inherent in all forms of life. Including the human. Even in us.

Everywhere you go in the southwestern deserts you come across drawings on the rocks, on the canyon walls. Some are inscribed into the rock—*petroglyphs*. Some are painted on the rock—*pictographs*. All of them, pictographs and petroglyphs alike, present an odd and so-far-untranslated language. If it is a language.

Not that the pictures are always hard to understand. Most consist of recognizable figures: deer, bighorn sheep, antelope, sometimes a mastodon (extinct no more than ten thousand years in North America), serpents, centipedes, rain clouds, the sun, dancing humans, warriors with shields and lances, even men on horseback—representations that cannot be more than four hundred years old, when the Spaniards introduced the horse to North America.

Some of the pictures, however, are disturbingly strange. We see semihuman figures with huge blank eyes, horned heads. Ghostly shapes resembling men, but without feet or legs, float on the air. Humanlike forms with helmets and goggles wave tentacles at us. What can they be? Gods? Goddesses? Cosmonauts from the Betelgeuse neighborhood? Here's a fighter with shield painted red, white and blue—the all-American man. And still other forms appear, completely nonrepresentational, totally abstract symbols of . . . of what? Nobody knows. The American Indians of today, if they know, aren't telling. Probably they are as mystified by them as we are. In any case the culture of the modern Native Americans has little connection with the culture of the vanished rock artists. The continuity was broken long ago.

But still we ask, what does the rock art mean? Unlike the story of the cliff ruins, fairly coherent to archaeologists, we know little of the significance of this ancient work. Perhaps it was only doodling of a sort. A bunch of Stone Age deer hunters sit in camp day after day with nothing to do (the game is gone), telling lies, chip-

ping arrowheads, straightening arrow shafts with their dough-
nutlike straightener stones. One of them, wanting to record his
lies for posterity, begins to chisel the image of a six-point buck on
the overhanging cliff wall. I killed that animal, he boasts, with my
bare hands.

Another liar takes up the challenge. I killed six bighorn rams,
he claims, in this very canyon, only fourteen years ago. And he
tallies the total on the soft sandstone with a hard-edged chunk of
agate or basalt or flint.

These shallow scratchings may have been the beginning. Inevitably the power of art took over. Most hunter-warriors were artists. They had to be. They made their own weapons. A weapon,
to be useful, has to be well made. A well-made weapon or any
well-made tool, when crafted by hand, becomes a work of art.

Perhaps the rock art was created by specialists. By shamans
and wizards, evoking sympathetic magic to aid the hunt. Portray-
ing a deer slain by an arrow, the medicine man would believe that
his wishes would serve as efficient cause in producing the desired
result. Imitative magic: life imitates art. Thus the pictographs and
petroglyphs may have had a religious denotation, hunting being
central to any hunter's religion.

The art served as a record. As practical magic. And as commu-
nication between wanderers. Water around the next bend, a certain zigzag sign might mean. We killed eleven bighorn here, only
two hundred years ago, says a second. *We were here, say the
hunters. We were here, say the artists.*

What about the spectral forms—the ghosts, ghouls, gods? Supernatural beings are fished from dreams. From the caves of Al-
tamira to the base of Ayers Rock in central Australia, all original,
aboriginal people have believed in the power of dreams. In the
Dream Time, say the wise old men of the outback, we made our
beginning; from the Dream Time we come; into the Dream Time,
after death, we shall return. The dream is the real; waking life is
only a dream within a greater dream.

These are speculations. Only a few anthropologists, like New Mexico's Dr. Polly Schaafsma, have given the Indian rock art serious attention. Most have observed the drawings, recorded them, but made no further study. At this time there is no method known by which the pictographs and petroglyphs can be dated accurately; dendrochronology (tree rings) and the carbon-14 technique cannot be applied here. Nor can the art be correlated with other archaeological data—cliff dwellings, burial sites, the various styles of pottery-, basket-, and toolmaking. In the absence of verifiable scientific information, the interpretation of rock art has been left by default to popular fancy: thus the early and premature labeling of this art as a form of "writing" or "hieroglyphs." Not surprising. The first reaction of anyone seeing these strange pictures for the first time is the naturally human: what do they *mean*?

Perhaps meaning is not of primary importance here. What is important is the recognition of art, wherever we may discover it, in whatever form. These canyon paintings and canyon inscriptions are valuable for their own sake, as work of elegance, freshness, originality (in the original sense of the word), economy of line, precision of point, integrity of materials. They are beautiful. And all of them are hundreds of years old—some may be much, much older.

The artist Paul Klee, whose surreal work resembles some of this desert rock art, wrote in his *Diaries 1898–1918*: "There are two mountains on which the weather is bright and clear, the mountain of the animals and the mountain of the gods. But between lies the shadowy valley of men." How's that for meaning?

On many walls in the desert we find the figure of the humpbacked flute player, Kokopelli (a Hopi name). A wanderer, for sure, and a man of strange powers, Kokopelli may have been the Pied Piper who led the cliff dwellers out of the canyons, out of their fear, and down to the high, open country to the south, where the people could live more like humans and less like bats.

Maybe he was a nomadic witch doctor, a healer of bodies and curer of feverishly imaginative savage souls. Nobody knows. The memory of the actual Kokopelli, if he was an actual person, has been lost. Only the outline of Kokopelli, his image chiseled into rock, has survived. Too bad. Many of us would like very much to hear the music that he played on that flute of his.

The American desert was discovered by an unknown people. They tried its deepest secrets. Now they have vanished, extinct as the tapir and the coryphodon. But the undeciphered message that they left us remains, written on the walls. A message preserved not in mere words and numbers but in the durable images of line on stone. *We were here.*

Language, in the mind of a poet, seeks to transcend itself, "to grasp the thing that has no name." It seems reasonable to suppose that the unknown people who left this record of their passage felt the same impulse toward permanence, the same longing for communion with the world that we feel today. To ask for any more meaning may be as futile as to ask for a meaning in the desert itself. What does the desert mean? It means what it is. It is there, it will be there when we are gone. But for a while we living things—men, women, birds, that coyote howling far off on yonder stony ridge—we were a part of it all. That should be enough.

FIVE

THE DAMNATION
OF A CANYON

There was a time when, in my search for essences, I concluded that the canyonland country has no heart. I was wrong. The canyonlands did have a heart, a living heart, and that heart was Glen Canyon and the golden, flowing Colorado River.

In the summer of 1959 a friend and I made a float trip in little rubber rafts down through the length of Glen Canyon, starting at Hite and getting off the river near Gunsight Butte—The Crossing of the Fathers. In this voyage of

95

some 150 miles and ten days our only motive power, and all that we needed, was the current of the Colorado River.

In the summer and fall of 1967 I worked as a seasonal park ranger at the new Glen Canyon National Recreation Area. During my five-month tour of duty I worked at the main marina and headquarters area called Wahweap, at Bullfrog Basin toward the upper end of the reservoir, and finally at Lee's Ferry downriver from Glen Canyon Dam. In a number of powerboat tours I was privileged to see almost all of our nation's newest, biggest and most impressive "recreational facility."

Having thus seen Glen Canyon both before and after what we may fairly call its damnation, I feel that I am in a position to evaluate the transformation of the region caused by construction of the dam. I have had the unique opportunity to observe first-hand some of the differences between the environment of a free river and a power-plant reservoir.

One should admit at the outset to a certain bias. Indeed I am a "butterfly chaser, googly eyed bleeding heart and wild conservative." I take a dim view of dams; I find it hard to learn to love cement; I am poorly impressed by concrete aggregates and statistics in the cubic tons. But in this weakness I am not alone, for I belong to that ever-growing number of Americans, probably a good majority now, who have become aware that a fully industrialized, thoroughly urbanized, elegantly computerized social system is not suitable for human habitation. Great for machines, yes. But unfit for people.

Lake Powell, formed by Glen Canyon Dam, is not a lake. It is a reservoir, with a constantly fluctuating water level—more like a bathtub that is never drained than a true lake. As at Hoover (or Boulder) Dam, the sole practical function of this impounded water is to drive the turbines that generate electricity in the powerhouse at the base of the dam. Recreational benefits were of secondary importance in the minds of those who conceived and built this dam. As a result the volume of water in the reservoir is continually being increased or decreased according to the requirements of the Basin States Compact and the power-grid system of which Glen Canyon Dam is a component.

The rising and falling water level entails various consequences. One of the most obvious, well known to all who have seen Lake Mead, is the "bathtub ring" left on the canyon walls after each drawdown of water, or what rangers at Glen Canyon call the Bathtub Formation. This phenomenon is perhaps of no more than aesthetic importance; yet it is sufficient to dispel any illusion one might have, in contemplating the scene, that you are looking upon a natural lake.

Of much more significance is the fact that plant life, because of the unstable water line, cannot establish itself on the shores of the reservoir. When the water is low, plant life dies of thirst; when high, it is drowned. Much of the shoreline of the reservoir consists of near-perpendicular sandstone bluffs, where very little flora ever did or ever could subsist, but the remainder includes bays, coves, sloping hills and the many side canyons, where the original plant life has been drowned and new plant life cannot get a foothold. And of course where there is little or no plant life there is little or no animal life.

The utter barrenness of the reservoir shoreline recalls by contrast the aspect of things before the dam, when Glen Canyon formed the course of the untamed Colorado. Then we had a wild and flowing river lined by boulder-strewn shores, sandy beaches, thickets of tamarisk and willow, and glades of cottonwoods.

The thickets teemed with songbirds: vireos, warblers, mockingbirds and thrushes. On the open beaches were killdeer, sandpipers, herons, ibises, egrets. Living in grottoes in the canyon walls were swallows, swifts, hawks, wrens and owls. Beaver were common if not abundant: not an evening would pass, in drifting down the river, that we did not see them or at least hear the whack of their flat tails on the water. Above the river shores were the great recessed alcoves where water seeped from the sandstone, nourishing the semitropical hanging gardens of orchid, ivy and columbine, with their associated swarms of insects and birdlife.

Up most of the side canyons, before damnation, there were springs, sometimes flowing streams, waterfalls and plunge pools —the kind of marvels you can now find only in such small-scale remnants of Glen Canyon as the Escalante area. In the rich flora of these laterals the larger mammals—mule deer, coyote, bobcat, ring-tailed cat, gray fox, kit fox, skunk, badger and others—found a home. When the river was dammed almost all of these things were lost. Crowded out—or drowned and buried under mud.

The difference between the present reservoir, with its silent sterile shores and debris-choked side canyons, and the original Glen Canyon, is the difference between death and life. Glen Canyon was alive. Lake Powell is a graveyard.

For those who may think I exaggerate the contrast between the former river canyon and the present man-made impoundment, I suggest a trip on Lake Powell followed immediately by another boat trip on the river below the dam. Take a boat from Lee's Ferry up the river to within sight of the dam, then shut off the motor and allow yourself the rare delight of a quiet, effortless drifting down the stream. In that twelve-mile stretch of living green, singing birds, flowing water and untarnished canyon walls—sights and sounds a million years older and infinitely lovelier than the roar of motorboats—you will rediscover a small and imperfect sampling of the kind of experience that was taken away from everybody when the oligarchs and politicians condemned our river for purposes of their own.

The effects of Glen Canyon Dam also extend downstream, causing changes in the character and ecology of Marble Gorge and Grand Canyon. Because the annual spring floods are now a thing of the past, the shores are becoming overgrown with brush, the rapids are getting worse where the river no longer has enough force to carry away the boulders washed down from the lateral canyons, and the beaches are disappearing, losing sand that is not replaced.

Lake Powell, though not a lake, may well be as its defenders assert the most beautiful reservoir in the world. Certainly it has a photogenic backdrop of buttes and mesas projecting above the expansive surface of stagnant waters where the speedboats, houseboats and cabin cruisers ply. But it is no longer a wilderness. It is no longer a place of natural life. It is no longer Glen Canyon.

The defenders of the dam argue that the recreational benefits available on the surface of the reservoir outweigh the loss of Indian ruins, historical sites, wildlife and wilderness adventure. Relying on the familiar quantitative logic of business and bureaucracy, they assert that whereas only a few thousand citizens ever ventured down the river through Glen Canyon, now millions can—or will—enjoy the motorized boating and hatchery fishing available on the reservoir. They will also argue that the rising waters behind the dam have made such places as Rainbow Bridge accessible by powerboat. Formerly you could get there only by walking (six miles).

This argument appeals to the wheelchair ethos of the wealthy, upper-middle-class American slob. If Rainbow Bridge is worth seeing at all, then by God it should be easily, readily, immediately available to everybody with the money to buy a big powerboat. Why should a trip to such a place be the privilege only of those who are willing to walk six miles? Or if Pikes Peak is worth getting to, then why not build a highway to the top of it so that anyone can get there? Anytime? Without effort? Or as my old man would say, "By Christ, one man's just as good as another—if not a damn sight better."

Or as ex-Commissioner Floyd Dominy of the U.S. Bureau of Reclamation pointed out poetically in his handsomely engraved and illustrated brochure *Lake Powell: Jewel of the Colorado* (produced by the U.S. Government Printing Office at our expense):

"There's something about a lake which brings us a little closer to God." In this case, Lake Powell, about five hundred feet closer. Eh, Floyd?

It is quite true that the flooding of Glen Canyon has opened up to the motorboat explorer parts of side canyons that formerly could be reached only by people able to walk. But the sum total of terrain visible to the eye and touchable by hand and foot has been greatly diminished, not increased. Because of the dam the river is gone, the inner canyon is gone, the best parts of the numerous side canyons are gone—all hidden beneath hundreds of feet of polluted water, accumulating silt, and mounting tons of trash. This portion of Glen Canyon—and who can estimate how many cubic miles were lost?—*is no longer accessible to anybody.* (Except scuba divers.) And this, do not forget, was the most valuable part of Glen Canyon, richest in scenery, archaeology, history, flora and fauna.

Not only has the heart of Glen Canyon been buried, but many of the side canyons above the fluctuating waterline are now rendered more difficult, not easier, to get into. This because the debris brought down into them by desert storms, no longer carried away by the river, must unavoidably build up in the area where flood meets reservoir. Narrow Canyon, for example, at the head of the impounded waters, is already beginning to silt up and to amass huge quantities of driftwood, some of it floating on the surface, some of it half afloat beneath the surface. Anyone who has tried to pilot a motorboat through a raft of half-sunken logs and bloated dead cows will have his own thoughts on the accessibility of these waters.

Hite Marina, at the mouth of Narrow Canyon, will probably have to be abandoned within twenty or thirty years. After that it will be the turn of Bullfrog Marina. And then Rainbow Bridge Marina. And eventually, inevitably, whether it takes ten centuries or only one, Wahweap. Lake Powell, like Lake Mead, is foredoomed sooner or later to become a solid mass of mud, and its dam a waterfall. Assuming, of course, that either one stands that long.

Second, the question of costs. It is often stated that the dam and its reservoir have opened up to the many what was formerly restricted to the few, implying in this case that what was once expensive has now been made cheap. Exactly the opposite is true.

Before the dam, a float trip down the river through Glen Canyon would cost you a minimum of seven days' time, well within anyone's vacation allotment, and a capital outlay of about forty dollars—the prevailing price of a two-man rubber boat with oars, available at any army-navy surplus store. A life jacket might be useful but not required, for there were no dangerous rapids in the 150 miles of Glen Canyon. As the name implies, this stretch of the river was in fact so easy and gentle that the trip could be and was made by all sorts of amateurs: by Boy Scouts, Camp Fire Girls, stenographers, schoolteachers, students, little old ladies in inner tubes. Guides, professional boatmen, giant pontoons, outboard motors, radios, rescue equipment were not needed. The Glen Canyon float trip was an adventure anyone could enjoy, on his own, for a cost less than that of spending two days and nights in a Page motel. Even food was there, in the water: the channel catfish were easier to catch and a lot better eating than the striped bass and rainbow trout dumped by the ton into the reservoir these days. And one other thing: at the end of the float trip you still owned your boat, usable for many more such casual and carefree expeditions.

What is the situation now? Float trips are no longer possible. The only way left for the exploration of the reservoir and what remains of Glen Canyon demands the use of a powerboat. Here you have three options: (1) buy your own boat and engine, the necessary auxiliary equipment, the fuel to keep it moving, the parts and repairs to keep it running, the permits and licenses required for legal operation, the trailer to transport it; (2) rent a boat; or (3) go on a commercial excursion boat, packed in with other sightseers, following a preplanned itinerary. This kind of play is only for the affluent.

The inescapable conclusion is that no matter how one attempts to calculate the cost in dollars and cents, a float trip down Glen Canyon was much cheaper than a powerboat tour of the reservoir. Being less expensive, as well as safer and easier, the float trip was an adventure open to far more people than will ever be able to afford motorboat excursions in the area now.

What about the "human impact" of motorized use of the Glen Canyon impoundment? We can visualize the floor of the reservoir gradually accumulating not only silt, mud, waterlogged trees and drowned cattle but also the usual debris that is left behind when the urban, industrial style of recreation is carried into the open country. There is also the problem of human wastes. The waters of the wild river were good to drink, but nobody in his senses would drink from Lake Powell. Eventually, as is already some-times the case at Lake Mead, the stagnant waters will become too foul even for swimming. The trouble is that while some boats have what are called "self-contained" heads, the majority do not; most sewage is disposed of by simply pumping it into the water. It will take a while, but long before it becomes a solid mass of mud Lake Powell ("Jewel of the Colorado") will enjoy a passing fame as the biggest sewage lagoon in the American Southwest. Most tourists will never be able to afford a boat trip on this reservoir, but everybody within fifty miles will be able to smell it.

All of the foregoing would be nothing but a futile exercise in nostalgia (so much water over the dam) if I had nothing construc-tive and concrete to offer. But I do. As alternate methods of power generation are developed, such as solar, and as the nation estab-lishes a way of life adapted to actual resources and basic needs, so that the demand for electrical power begins to diminish, we can shut down the Glen Canyon power plant, open the diversion tun-nels, and drain the reservoir.

This will no doubt expose a drear and hideous scene: immense mud flats and whole plateaus of sodden garbage strewn with dead trees, sunken boats, the skeletons of long-forgotten, decomposing water-skiers. But to those who find the prospect too appalling, I say give nature a little time. In five years, at most in ten, the sun and wind and storms will cleanse and sterilize the repellent mess. The inevitable floods will soon remove all that does not belong within the canyons. Fresh green willow, box elder and redbud will reappear; and the ancient drowned cottonwoods (noble monuments to themselves) will be replaced by young of their own kind. With the renewal of plant life will come the insects, the birds, the lizards and snakes, the mammals. Within a generation—thirty years—I predict the river and canyons will bear a decent resemblance to their former selves. Within the lifetime of our children Glen Canyon and the living river, heart of the canyonlands, will be restored to us. The wilderness will again belong to God, the people and the wild things that call it home.

SIX

A COLORADO RIVER
JOURNAL

Bright-eyed and bushy-tailed, ready to run the wild waters of the Grand Canyon, we assemble at Lee's Ferry, Arizona, on the banks of the brand-new cold green Colorado River. Green because of microplankton. Cold because this water is issuing from the bottom of a dam twelve miles upstream—that Glen Canyon Dam. The temperature of the water here is forty-seven degrees Fahrenheit. (I place a six-pack of Michelob in the water for quick chilling.) And brand new? This river is not the Colorado we knew and loved. The real Colorado died in 1964 when the engineers of the Bureau of Reclamation closed the gates at Glen Canyon Dam, changing the Colorado from a wild and free river into the domesticated, well-regulated conveyor belt for baloney boats that it is today.

And who are "we"? Well, there's boatman and photographer John Blaustein, loading his little wooden dory called *Peace River*. He looks anxious. Can't blame him. He has many problems on his mind—cameras, the passengers, the rapids.

His boss, one Martin Litton, who owns and manages Grand Canyon Dories, is hanging around nearby. Years ago I was the ranger here at Lee's Ferry. I used to squeeze Martin's life jackets, testing them for safety.

"Look here, Martin," I say, giving one of his flimsy boats a kick in the slats, "you don't really expect us to float down the river and run the rapids in a thing like this. What's it made of, plywood? One rap on a rock and it'll crack like an egg." Talking of old times and new problems, he ignores my facetious fears.

I turn my attention to the other boatmen and to my fellow passengers on this suicidal journey down the river of no return.

There are seven dories, bright, elegant, fragile, gaily painted craft, each named after some natural feature destroyed or maimed by the works of man: the *Peace River* (dammed in Canada); *Tapestry Wall, Moqui Steps, Music Temple* (lovely places in Glen Canyon now sunk beneath the stagnant waters of Lake Powell National Sewage Lagoon); the *Vale of Rhondda* (a mine-ravaged valley in Wales); and the *Columbia* and the *Celilo Falls* (drowned by the Dalles Dam on the Columbia River). The boats are about seventeen feet long from stem to transom, seven feet wide at the beam. Closed hatches at bow, midships, and stern make them "virtually" unsinkable, we are told. Why "virtually"? What sinister ambiguities are contained in that sly equivocation? Why not say "virtually floatable"? How about "virtually sunk," "virtually drowned," or "virtually dead"?

And the boatmen, they look more dangerous than the boats. Seven little wooden boats and seven furtive, grinning boatmen with fourteen hairy, crooked legs. They look like overgrown gnomes. I feel like Snow White, stumbling into the wrong fairy tale. A Disneyfied nightmare. Time to back out of this deal. I knew there was something queer about the whole setup, this supposedly free ride on the new Grand Canyon subway. Be wiser to hike it, maybe, stepping from boat to boat all the way to Lake Mead, our destination, 277 miles downstream.

I'm looking for a way to creep off unnoticed when my escape is interdicted by the approach of two of my twenty or so fellow passengers. Some fellows. One is a brown exotic wench in a tiger-skin bikini; she has the eyes and hair of Salome. The other is a tall slim trim sloop of a girl with flaxen hair and perfect sateen thighs emerging from the skimpiest pair of Levi cutoffs I have ever seen. I pause, hesitate, reconsider. One of the two is Renée—my wife. But which?

Following my bowsprit back to the beach, I join the crowd around Wally Rist, the head boatman, who is demonstrating—on the exotic Salome—the proper way to fasten a life jacket.

Minutes later, all too soon, without adequate spiritual preparation, we are launched forth on the mad and complex waters of the frigid river. John Blaustein has cajoled me into his dory, making certain I do not slip off at the last moment.

We pass through the Paria Riffle without upset, much to everyone's relief, as John strains at the oars. Nine years earlier, when I was ranger here, I took my girl friends for rides down these riffles, whacking the waves with a Park Service motorboat. How many propellers did I mangle that summer, pivoting off rocks and driving blindly into unobserved gravel bars? Three or four. (Too much beer, too little bikini.)

A nice runoff comes in from the Paria River, staining the Colorado a healthy hue of brown. Anything, any color—Day-Glo purple, chartreuse, shocking pink—is better than the unnatural translucent green, like Gatorade, of our river as it comes strained through the penstocks of Glen Canyon Dam.

We pass the little beach where, years before, I used to lie on the sand and watch my favorite birds—turkey vultures, shrikes, ruby-throated hummingbirds, rosy-bottomed skinnydippers. Above, on a windswept sunbaked stony bench under the mighty Vermilion Cliffs, is the new Park Service all-metal campground, packed with Winnebagos, house trailers, pickup-campers, trail bikes, jeeps, motorboats and the other paraphernalia necessary to a holiday in the wilds. Four miles downriver from Lee's Ferry we glide beneath Navajo Bridge, 467 feet above. As the canyon walls rise on either side, a new rock formation appears—the Kaibab limestone.

This is Marble Gorge, beginning of the Grand Canyon. Entering here over a century ago, Major John Wesley Powell wrote as follows in his diary:

August 5, 1869—With some feeling of anxiety we enter a new canyon this morning. We have learned to observe closely the texture of the rock. In softer strata we have a quiet river, in harder we find rapids and falls. Below us are the limestones and hard sandstones which we found in Cataract Canyon. This bodes toil and danger.

Toil and danger. Don't care for the sound of those words. Danger is bad enough; toil is reprehensible. Hope these savage-looking boatmen know what they're doing. They certainly don't look as though they know what they're doing. Of course I've been down here before. Used to drive the Park Service motorboat as far as Mile 8, Badger Creek Rapid, and twice went all the way down the canyon on a big motor-driven pontoon boat.

The canyon deepens, forming walls that cut off most of the sky. We float through a monstrous defile a thousand feet deep, two thousand feet deep? How deep is the river? one of the passengers asks John. How high are the walls? How fast is the current? The traditional questions. He answers patiently. What's that great blue heronlike bird down there that flies like a pterodactyl?

John tells us that the canyon is nearly all rock. How much can you say about rock? It's red here, gray there, it's hard, it's badly eroded, it's a mess. The geologists can't even make up their minds how the canyon was formed. They once thought it was an entrenched meander, the ancient silt-bearing river grinding down into its bed as the plateau gradually rose beneath it. Now some think it's the result of two rivers, one capturing the other in the vicinity of the present Little Colorado. Old-time geologists spoke of a monster cataclysm. One thing is certain: the Grand Canyon is *the canyon*.

Now from up ahead comes the deep toneless vibration of the first major rapid, Badger Creek. The sound resembles that of an approaching freight train on a steel trestle. On the standard scale of 1 to 10 this rapid is rated 4–6. Of intermediate difficulty. Staring, we see the river come to an edge and vanish. Curling waves leap, from time to time, above that edge. Wally Rist, in the leading boat, stands up for a good look, sits down, turns his boat, and facing forward, slides over the glassy rim of water. His boat disappears. He disappears. Two more boats follow. They disappear. Our turn.

"Buckle up," commands John.

We fasten our life jackets. John stands up in the center of the boat, taking his look. Pooled behind the wall of boulders that forms the rapid, the river slows, moving with sluggish ease toward the dropoff. The roar grows louder. I think of Pittsburgh, old Forbes Field, seventh game of the 1960 World Series, bottom of the ninth, score tied, 9–9, and the roar that greeted Bill Mazeroski's Series-winning homer. A roar that lasted for two weeks.

Wake up. Daydreaming. John has seated himself; the bow of the dory is sliding down the oily tongue of the rapid, holes and boils and haystack waves exploding around us. John makes a perfect run straight down the middle. One icy wave reaches up and slaps me in the chest, drenches my belly. *Cold!* The shock of it. But we are through, easy, riding the choppy tailwaves of the rapid. John catches the bottom of the eddy on the right and with a few deft strokes brings our boat to the beach at the mouth of Badger Creek. The other boats join us. Boatmen and passengers clamber ashore. Here we'll make camp for our first night on the river. True, we haven't gone far, but then, we didn't get started till noon.

Setting up camp for the night is a routine chore for the boatmen. All food supplies for the eighteen days and personal belongings are neatly packed into the watertight compartments below the decks of the boats. The large cans of food are packed first, their weight on the bottom of the boat adding stability for the rapids. Next go large waterproof containers with things like bread, eggs and flour, and army-surplus rubber bags for clothing and sleeping gear. Cameras and small personal gear are carried in surplus ammunition cans.

Most of the passengers line up behind the boats to retrieve their rubber bags and immediately disperse up the beach to find a flat spot in the sand on which to set up their camps. There is an ample supply of semiprivate nooks and crannies among the tamarisk trees, so I see no reason to rush, and decide instead to have a cold beer.

One of the boatmen, the one they call Sharky, a fiercely bearded lad with burning blue eyes, is in charge of toilet facilities. In the old days passengers and crew simply dispersed to the bushes, women upstream, men downstream. Now that the canyon is so popular, however, with some fifteen thousand souls per summer riding through, it has become necessary for sanitary and aesthetic reasons to make use of portable chemical toilets. Sharky (junior member of the crew) is our porta-potty porter. He removes the unit from his boat and sets it up among the shady tamarisk far from the beach, in a spot with a pleasant view of the river and canyon walls. He is the kind who thinks of such things. Later, some of the passengers will wander around half the night hunting for it.

The boatmen set up the "stove"—a metal box, filled with dry driftwood and covered with a steel grate. The cooks begin at once preparing supper. Our cooks are two able and handsome young women named Jane Whalen and Kenly Weills. Both are competent oarswomen as well and can substitute for the boatmen if necessary.

Drinking water is taken right from the river and chemically purified. If the water is extra muddy, lime and alum are added to settle it.

After dinner—pork chops, applesauce, salad, soup, peaches, coffee, tea, et cetera (the "et cetera" in my case being a bit of Ron Rico 151)—we are subjected to a lecture by Head Boatman Wally. Now that they've taken our money and gotten us down here beyond reach of civilization, he talks about the realities of Grand Canyon life: how to use the portable toilet unit (no simple matter); about cactus, scorpions, centipedes and "buzzworms" (rattlesnakes); about loose rocks and broken bones; quicksand, whirlpools and asphyxiation; the remoteness of medical aid. Wally instructs us in what to do if a boat tips over, as it sometimes does; tells us the hazards of diving into the river and swimming in the current.

We pay scant attention to all that rot and soon afterward Sharky digs out his recorder, his ukulele and his kazoo and announces a porta-potty porter's party. Bottles appear. Darkness settles in, decorum decays. Salome dances in the sand.

One more nip on the Ron Rico and two more songs and then I slink away. I unroll my sleeping bag, but the air is so warm I hardly need to crawl into it. By dawn I will. Two shooting stars trace lingering parabolas of blue fire across the sky. From below rises the sound of rowdy, unseemly music. Crickets chirp. The steady, rhythmic rumble of the river pouring over the rocks is marvelously soothing. I soon drop off to sleep.

𝄐

A cool morning, overcast sky.

More birds for somebody's life list: brown-headed cowbird, western tanager, black-necked stilts, violet-green swallows, black-throated swifts. The swifts like to skim close to the waves in the rapids, attracted, it would seem, by the turbulent air. According to Rich Turner, one of our boatmen, they sometimes hit the waves and drown.

The river is rising but not fast enough. Boatmen get nervous about running the serious rapids with insufficient water. Those rocks, those granite fangs foaming with froth in the charging stream. Bad dreams.

We push onto a river the color of bronze, shimmering like hammered metal under the desert sun. Through Unkar Rapid—made it! Then 75 Mile Rapid (4–7). Still alive. We pull ashore above Hance Rapid (7–8) for study and consultation.

Hance is always a problem for the dorymen, especially in low water. Just too many goddamned rocks sticking up, or even worse, half hidden near the surface. No clear route through. A zigzag course. Huge waves, treacherous boils, churning holes that can eat a boat alive. A kind of slalom course for oarsmen, with the penalty for a mistake a possible smashed boat. The big advantage of rubber boats is that they can usually be bounced off the well-polished boulders in the rapids without suffering damage. Usually. But rigid craft such as dories or kayaks may split, puncture, crack like an eggshell. Therefore their safe passage through a big rapid—through any rapid—requires highly skilled maneuvering on the part of the man at the oars.

The boatmen stand on high points beside the rapid, study the obstacles, consult among themselves. We, the passengers, are herded downriver along the shore by Kenly and Jane, the cooks, and assembled below the rapid. The boatmen are going through this one without us. The boats will be lighter and will draw less water, making them more maneuverable. None of the passengers seems to object to this arrangement. Most of them are busy loading their cameras.

The boatmen run it without us, one by one, not easily but safely. We rejoin our boats. The river carries us swiftly into the Granite Gorge. Like a tunnel of love, there are no shores or beaches in here. The burnished and river-sculptured rocks rise sheer from the water's edge, cutting off all view of the higher cliffs, all of the outer world but a winding column of blue sky. We race along as in a gigantic millstream. As usual, Powell described the scene as well as anyone ever will:

August 14, 1869—The gorge is black and narrow below, red and gray and flaring above, with crags and angular projections on the walls. . . . Down in these grand gloomy depths we glide, ever listening, ever watching.

Grand, we'd agree, but not gloomy. *Glowing* is the word. The afternoon sun is hidden by the narrow walls, but indirect light, reflected and refracted by the water, by the pink granitic sills and dikes in the polished cliffs, by the blue lenses of the atmosphere, streams upon us from many angles, all radiant. However, unlike Powell and his men, we are fresh, well fed, well supplied, secure in our bulging life jackets, confident in our dories, too ignorant (except the boatmen) for fear.

Two miles below Hance we crash through the well-named Sockdolager Rapid (5–7), and two and a half miles later into and through Grapevine Rapid (6–7), both so named by Major Powell. Litton's buoyant boats ride high on the waves but not high enough to escape the recoil of the descending fifty-two-degree waters. Screams of delight, shock, astonishment, ring through the canyon as we ride this undulating roller coaster. Unlike the sea, here on the river the water moves, the waves remain in place, waiting for us. Soaked and chilled, we bail out the boats and watch mysterious glenlike tributary canyons pass by on either side. Asbestos Canyon (remains of an old mine up there), Vishnu Creek, Lonetree Canyon, Clear Creek, Zoroaster Canyon, Cremation Creek (what happened there? No one in our party knows), and others. In the early afternoon we pull ashore at Phantom Ranch for rest and refreshment.

Phantom Ranch, combination ranger station and tourist hostel, is the only outpost of civilization within the canyon. From here broad and well-maintained foot and mule trails lead to both the North and South Rims. Also a telephone line. And a waterline, built at taxpayers' expense, for the benefit of the motel industry on the South Rim. There is even a clearing for helicopters. The two footbridges over the river are the only Colorado River crossings from Navajo Bridge to Hoover Dam.

Here we pause for an hour. Some of the passengers are departing us at this point, having contracted for only the first part of the voyage. Their places are taken by others who have hiked the trail down from South Rim. We are ready. One by one the boats shove off, deeper into the inner gorge.

This time my wife and I sit in the bow of the leading dory. Our boatman is young Rich Turner—musician, ornithologist, schoolteacher, rock climber, high diver, veteran oarsman, one of Litton's most experienced hands. Two other passengers are on board— Jane the cook and a newcomer, fifteen-year-old Jenny, a girl from Henderson, Kentucky. Active, athletic Jenny has never been on a river trip of any kind before. As we drift down the river, Rich plying the oars at a leisurely pace, she asks us if we don't get bored sometimes with this effortless mode of travel. Sure we do, but none of us will admit it. We tell her about the birds and the interesting geological formations; the pleasant afternoons in the cool shade, with the sun setting on the high canyon walls; the contrast of the quiet beauty of the side canyons with the violent crashing roar of the rapids.

Rich suggests that we buckle life jackets. Horn Creek Rapid (7–9) coming up, he reminds us. He says something about The Great Wave. For Jenny's benefit he reviews routine upset procedures: take deep breath when entering rapids; hang on; if boat turns over, get out from under and grab lifeline strung along gunwales; stay on upstream side of boat to avoid being crushed between boat and a hard place; climb up onto bottom of boat as soon as possible; grasp flip line and assist boatman in righting boat; bail out water; relax and enjoy the view.

"What was that about a great wave?" Renée asks.

"I didn't say 'a' great wave," says Rich. "I said '*The* Great Wave.'"

More boatman's hype—short for hyperbole. Dorymen love to melodramatize the peril of the rapids. Makes their idyllic jobs seem important, gives the gullible passenger the illusion that he's getting his money's worth.

Comes the now-familiar growing roar of uproarious waters. Not far ahead the river plays its usual conjuring trick, seeming to pour over the edge of the known world and disappear down into some kind of grumbling abyss. Above the watery rim I can see hints of a rainbow in the mist, backlit by the westering sun. We've seen this sort of thing before.

What I've forgotten is that Horn, unlike the longer rapids above and below, makes its descent abruptly, in one dive, through a constricted channel where the river is squeezed into sudden acceleration. Rich stands up for a last look but sits down quickly. The boat slides down the glassy tongue of the current. Into a yawning mouth. I take a deep breath—involuntarily. "Hang on!" Rich shouts.

The dory plunges down into the watery hole, then up the slope of the standing wave. Water topples upon us, filling the boat in an instant. But momentum carries us through the first wave and into a second, deeper, hole. "One more!" Rich yells, his oars stroking empty air. We climb into a second wave, taller than the first. It hangs above my head, a rippling, translucent, golden liquid wall. Our sluggish boat plows through it.

"And one more!" cries Rich. One more indeed. The dory drops into the deepest hole yet. I think I can almost see bedrock bottom. The third wave towers above us. Far above. The Great Wave. Heavily our water-loaded boat, askew, climbs up its face. Never makes it. As the wave breaks upon us from the port side our dory turns over with the solemn, grave, inevitable certainty of disaster. No one says a word as we go under.

Below the surface all is silent and dark. Part of the current, I do not even feel a sense of motion. But before there is time to think or feel much about anything, the life jacket brings me to the top. The dory, upside down, is only a stroke away. I grab the lifeline. Renée is hanging on beside me. And Rich and Jenny near the stern, Jane on the other side. The wrong side.

The river carries us swiftly toward the sheer canyon wall below the rapid, on the left. Jane seems a bit dazed like the rest of us, unaware of her danger. Rich pulls himself onto the flat bottom of the boat and drags her up with him. The boat crunches into the rock. Sound of splintering plywood. The weight of the current forces down the upstream side of the boat, pushing Renée and me underwater again. Down in the darkness I let go of the boat's lifeline and kick away.

After what seems an unnecessarily long time I rise to the surface, gasping for air. A wave splashes in my face. Good God, I'm drowning, I think, choking on a windpipe full of muddy water. Instinctively I swim toward shore and find myself caught in a big eddy, pulled in a circle by the swirling current.

Where's Renée? I see the boat go sailing past, upside down, three people crawling on it, none of them my wife. The eddy carries me close to the wall, and I make a futile effort to find a handhold on the glossy, polished stone. I give up and let the eddy carry me down again, toward a tumble of broken rock fallen from the wall. I succeed in getting onto the rocks and stand up, free of the hungry river at last.

Renée? I hear her calling me. Ah, there she is, below me on an adjoining shelf of rock. Reunited, we stand on our island in the stream and watch Rich, Jane, Jenny and the capsized dory float away, getting smaller and smaller. Forgetting for the moment that there are six other dories still up the river, feeling abandoned, we are delighted to see good John Blaustein come charging through The Great Wave. He picks us up. With six soaked passengers aboard, he rows hard after Rich and catches him. Rich is having trouble righting his boat. Not enough weight. John and I assist, pulling on the flip lines, and the boat comes over right side up again. Renée and I return to Rich's dory.

Rich rows, Renée and Jane and I bail. We open the hatches—not quite watertight after all—and bail them out too. Resting at last, we finally become aware of how chilled we are, through and through. Nobody timed it, but we must have been immersed in that frigid water for a considerable spell. Even the sun seems slow in bringing warmth back to our bones.

That evening in camp, as Rich patches up his injured dory with glue and fiberglass and yards of duct tape, it dawns on me why the boatmen sometimes refer to the major rapids as Christian Falls. Why? Because they make a believer out of you.

In the morning the river is low. John looks grim. I check the oracle rock. High and dry, and the river dropping slowly. That is bad news.

Breakfast is finished. We load the dories. Some of the boatmen are concerned that their boats are too light, since most of the food is gone. They place large rocks in the bottom of the hatches for ballast. The extra weight down low may help at Lava Falls, not far ahead. The worst rapid on the river.

August 13, 1869—What falls there are, we know not; what rocks beset the channel, we know not; what walls rise over the river, we know not. . . . The men talk as cheerfully as ever; jests are bandied about freely this morning; but to me the cheer is somber and the jests are ghastly.

Write on, good Major Powell. How prescient you were. I know exactly how you felt. I can read your every emotion on the face of John Blaustein.

We push off. Sunlight sparkles on the laughing wavelets of the master stream. Little birds twitter in the tamarisk.

It looks like a good day to die. All days are good, but this one looks better than most.

As Sharky pulls us into the current, lashing about lustily with the oars, I glance back at the beach we are departing. Only once. A black shadow lies across the unwet rugosities of oracle rock.

The highest sheer walls in the canyon rear above our heads. Two thousand feet straight up. With terraces and further higher walls beyond. Toroweap Overlook rises at Mile 176, three thousand feet above the river. The suicide's lodestone. We float beneath it.

When I worked at Grand Canyon, a young English major from Yale, unlucky in love, drove his car all the way from New Haven, Connecticut, to jump from Toroweap Overlook. Would have more class, he thought, than the banal routine off Golden Gate Bridge. Arriving here, he took one good look down into our awful chasm ("Gaze not too long into the abyss/Lest the abyss gaze into thee"—F. Nietzsche), walked back to his car (1970 Chevrolet Impala Supersport), attached a vacuum-cleaner hose to the tail pipe, ran the other end of the hose into the car, started the motor and gassed himself to death. While gassing he wrote a note explaining his procedure; also a final poem on life, death and the bitterness of youth that the critics agreed was not very good. It begins:

I came to Toroweap today
To look, to laugh, to leap away
From all these cares of mortal clay;
I looked—and found a better way. . . .

You see the fatal flaws. Inept alliteration. Heavy-handed rhyme scheme. Iambic tetrameter—wrong foot for elegies ("Foot like a hand."). Cliché filter not functioning. Sorry, lad, you'll have to do better than that. *C-minus.*

The river slides seaward in its stony groove. Will never make it. Mojave Desert–type vegetation now—mesquite, ocotillo, cat's-claw acacia, barrel cactus, clock-face and cowtongue prickly pear adorn as best they can the talus slopes below the cliffs. Names, names, the naming of the names. What's this? What's that? they ask me, pointing to this bush, that bush. I give my standard reply: What it *is*, ma'am, no one knows; but men call it—creosote bush.

We stop for lunch at Mile 177, not far above *that riffle*, from which point we can see the first remnants of the lava flows. Major Powell loved the scene:

August 25, 1869—What a conflict of water and fire there must have been here! Just imagine a river of molten rock running down into a river of melted snow. What a seething and boiling of the waters; what clouds of steam rolled into the heavens!

Looking solemn, head boatman Rist gives his final harangue of the trip.

"Listen!" he begins.

We listen. Don't hear a damn thing. Sigh of the river maybe, swooning round the next bend. Cicada keening in the dry grass.

Faint scream of the sun, ninety-three million miles above. Nothing significant.

"You don't hear it but it's there," he says. "Lava Falls (ten plus)." Mile 179. "It's always there. Every time we come down this river there it is. Drops thirty-seven feet in two hundred yards. The greatest rapid in North America. So we're gonna need help from you people. Anybody who's hoping to see a disaster, please stay out of sight. All passengers will walk around this one except volunteers. Yes, we'll need—"

Hands are rising.

"Not yet," Wally says. "We want everybody to see it first. Anybody who thinks he or she wants to ride through Lava has to get down there and walk below it and look up through the waves. Then you decide if you really want to do it. We want people who can handle the oars, who can help right the boat if it flips, and who can climb around on wet boulders if necessary. Nobody has to do it, but I'll tell you this much: when you're out there in the middle of Lava, it's nice to hear another heart beating besides your own. *But nobody has to do it*. Nobody has to prove anything—to himself or us. OK? From everybody else, we ask maximum moral support, as before, only more so. After Lava we'll have a party. Any questions?"

Commander Wally's briefing. You'd think we were in a U-boat about to enter a combat zone. Walter Rist—there is something Teutonic about that chap. The straight blond hair. The Nordic nostrils. The sardonic grin. I glance furtively up and down the river, trapped but not yet panicked. Where is that place? That Separation Canyon? That exit from this Hall of Horrors?

Salami on rye, potato salad, peanut butter and Ry-Krisp for lunch. Not half bad. It's all bad. The condemned man revealed no emotion as he ate his lunch. Ironic laughter in the background. No place to hide. Once more into your britches, friends. All boats shove off, loaded, onto the shining Colorado.

At Mile 178 a great black basaltic rock appears, standing silent in the middle of the river. Vulcan's Anvil, they call it. It looks like a forty-foot tombstone. Staring at it, we hear this weird whimpering noise from midships. Sharky singing his Martian funeral song. Wordless, it rises and falls in hemidemisemitones of unearthly misery. The dirge of the damned.

A muttering sound ahead, beyond the next bend. Wordless voices grumbling in subterranean echo chambers. All boats put ashore on the right bank. Wally leads us, passengers and crew, up a path through the tamarisk jungle and onto a slide of volcanic boulders big as bungalows, high above the river. Lava Falls bellows in the sunlight. He stops. We stop. He waves us on. "Volunteers will assemble here," he shouts, above the tumult from below. "*After* you've looked it over."

We go on, all but the boatmen, who remain clustered around Wally, commencing their customary hopeless confabulations. The sad smiles, the weary head-shakings. Same old hype. I smile too, slinking away.

Relieved, I join the sensible passengers, who gather in a safe shady place near the foot of the uproar. Breathing easily now, I watch these people ready their cameras. Comfortable, we consider the dancing falls, the caldron of colliding superwaves, the lava rocks like iron-blue bicuspids protruding from the foam—here, there, most everywhere, a fiendish distribution of dory-rending fangs. I study the channel on the far left—nothing but teeth. The "slot" in the middle: gone. Hah, I think, they're going to have to run it on the right. Right up against this basalt boxcar I'm relaxing on.

Time passes. Can't see the boatmen from here. I look back up at the "volunteers'" assembly point. Sure enough, a few suckers have showed up, seven or eight of them. And that tall girl in the big hat . . . my wife? It is my wife. Good Lord, what's she doing there?

Not all the boatmen are in hiding. John Blaustein crouches on a rock nearby, staring up at the rapids, his battery of cameras dangling from his neck. Like me, he's doing what we're supposed to do—*observe*.

A red, white and yellow dory appears on the tongue of the rapid, upstream. It's the *Tapestry Wall*. There's Captain Wally standing on his seat, one hand shielding his eyes. Two passengers with him, sunk deep in their seats, clutch with white knuckles at the gunwales. Wally lowers himself into the cockpit, takes a firm grip on the oars. Here they come. They disappear. They emerge, streaming with water. Dive and disappear again. Dark forms barely visible through the foam. The boat rears up into sunlight. Wally has crabbed an oar, lost an oarlock. He's in trouble. He's struggling with something. They vanish again, under the waves, to reappear not twenty feet from where I sit, bearing hard upon this immovable barrier. The dory yaws to port; Wally is standing up; he's only got one oar, looks as if he's trying to climb right out of the boat onto my rock. I'm about to offer a hand when I realize he's climbing the high side, preventing the boat from capsizing. Cushioned by a roil of water, the boat and its three occupants rush past me, only inches from the iron rock. Who's that lass in the stern, smiling bravely, waving one little brown paw at me? Renée! The violent current bears them away, out of sight.

Jesus . . .

One made it. Six more to go. We have to sit and watch this? Too late now, here comes Dane Mensik at the control console of the *Vale of Rhondda*. A passenger in the bow. He makes a perfect run, bow first through the holes, over the big waves, and clears Death Rock by a safe and sane three feet. And after him Mike Davis in the *Music Temple*. Likewise, a perfect run.

Three safely past, four to go. Now come in quick succession Sharky Cornell in the *Columbia*, Mike "Scorpion" Markovich in the *Moqui Steps*, and Rich Turner in the patched-up *Celilo Falls*. With a light payload of ballast—one passenger each—they make it right side up, one way or the other way, through the sound and fury of Mile 179.

Thank God . . .

Only one to go, and that has to be poor old John Blaustein in the ill-named *Peace River*. I glance up at the volunteers' assembly point. The slave block. One little girl stands there clutching her life jacket, hopefully waiting. No, it can't be. Yes, it is, it's Jenny, the kid who changed our luck at Horn Creek. The innocent Jonah. Now I really feel sorry for John. Not only are the scales of probability weighing against him—for if six made it through, the seventh is doomed for certain—but he and he alone has to ride with that sweet little jinx we picked up at Phantom Ranch. Tough luck, John. Kismet, you know. Bad karma. (But better him than me.)

Where is John, by the way?

I feel a firm hand on my shoulder. "Let's go," he says.

Well, of course I knew from the start it would turn out like this. I never had a chance.

We trudge up the rocks, pick up Jenny, trudge through the jungle and down to the lonely boat, hyperventilating all the way. Buckle up. John gives stern instructions, which I don't hear. Push off. Me and little Jenny in the bow. The sun glares at us over the oily water, blazing in our eyes. John points the boat the wrong way, right down the tongue into the heart of the madness. The moment of total commitment. This is absurd. We dive head first into the boiling waters . . .

Twenty seconds and it's over. Twenty seconds of total truth, and then we're cruising through the tail of the rapid, busy with the bailers, joining the procession of dories before us. Nothing to it. Running the big rapids is like sex: half the fun lies in the anticipation. Two-thirds of the thrill comes with the approach. The remainder is only ecstasy—or darkness.

On the beach. The moon is shining bright. The boatmen, armed with heavy grog, are having a private "debriefing" session downstream somewhere. Lewd silhouettes prance before our fire. Salome dances. Inhibitions fall like dandruff. Our four French passengers are finally speaking with our two Austrian passengers. The others—a twenty-three-year-old schoolteacher; a newspaper publisher, his wife, and three kids; a stockbroker; a retired lawyer; a dental hygienist; a physician—go over and over the events of the day. No one seems to be able to agree on what happened exactly during those twenty seconds in Lava Falls. No matter; we made it alive.

Dinner is served, vaguely. The seven merry boatmen stagger up from the lower beach, smiling and content. The sense of exhilaration and victory lasts all through the night.

SEVEN

ON THE HIGH EDGE
OF TEXAS

 *From Guadalupe Peak in Guadalupe Moun-
tains National Park, 8,751 feet above sea level, highest
point in what Texans call the largest unfrozen state in the
United States, we peer south through haze and wind
toward Mexico and the Sierra Madre—the Mother Mountains, obscured by dust and distance. We do have a good
view of the Pecos Valley to the east, dry salt lakes to the
west, the mountains of New Mexico to the northwest. And
the harsh bright blue of the sky overhead.*

West Texas—high lonesome country. Arid plains, glaring salt flats, rough and rugged desert mountains, bitter winds, snow in winter, heat and drought in summer, and all of it a long, long way from anywhere. El Paso lies 110 miles to the west, Carlsbad, New Mexico, 55 miles to the northeast, Pecos 80 miles southeast, and tiny Van Horn 55 miles south. There is nothing much in between these towns but creosote brush, saltbush, lizards, bats, jackrabbits, vultures and rattlesnakes—at least four species of rattlesnakes. Plus anomalous mountains rising like islands from the vast Chihuahuan Desert. And a few tough Texans, a few even tougher beef cattle. (Chop with cleavers, marinate in rotgut whisky and rat piss, chew with steel dentures—that's the local recipe for Son of a Bitch Stew.)

Such an environment breeds a cantankerous variety of human. For instance: I was told of the former owner and operator of a gasoline station near Pine Springs, on the eastern edge of Guadalupe Park, who refused to sell gasoline to strangers if the stranger's car failed to carry Texas license plates. Why? Well, for the main and simple reason that foreigners had no business nosing around Pine Springs, Texas.

Another story: About four years ago a local rancher, James Prather, seventy-nine years old, was riding alone in the rocky foothills looking for a cow, when he had an accident—his horse stumbled, broke its leg and rolled on top of the old man. The fall broke one of Prather's legs, a few ribs, and trapped him beneath the twelve-hundred-pound body of the horse. The horse, alive though crippled, kept thrashing about. The old man drew his revolver and shot the horse dead. Then he unholstered his knife and cut his way free from the carcass. He rested for a while before crawling three miles over rock, through brush and cactus, to the nearest road. He waited there for two days without food or water until somebody came along in a pickup truck. The old rancher was in a rage because nobody had found him sooner.

Such people do not adapt easily to the tourist business; Guadalupe Mountains National Park, established in 1971, is still regarded as an imposition and affront by many of its human-type neighbors.

Up here on the peak, though, we are untroubled by hostile natives. In fact, I can't see anybody around in any direction. The registration log testifies that quite a few others have been here, mostly Texans out to climb their highest mountain, but they aren't in sight today. Can't blame them. The wind, cold even in July, whistling, unrelenting, discourages loitering. Even worse is the heat, ninety-eight degrees Fahrenheit down below in the desert when we began this climb.

It wasn't easy getting here, but I suppose it was worth it. The route up, through Pine Spring Canyon, climbs three thousand feet in five miles. The trail is old, dim, primitive, little more than a deer path, the route marked by stone cairns. My wife and I each carried a gallon canteen; we drank half our water on the way up.

Standing here looking south we feel as if we're on the bridge of a great stone ship. The Guadalupe Mountain Range is wedge- or V-shaped, with this peak near the apex of the V. One mile to the south, seven hundred feet lower, is the actual apex, the bow of the ship, a spectacular escarpment called El Capitan. From that point the world drops away for an impressive two thousand feet straight down. You could drop a stone from rim to talus slope below without the stone touching anything but air. An exhilarating fall for acrophiles, a challenge for climbers, reminding me of Yosemite. But Guadalupe's rock walls are of ancient, corroded and rotten limestone, not sandstone or granite. The park regulations make the point: "Do not climb the cliffs. The limestone is unstable and considered unsafe even for technical climbers." Even a bat might hesitate to walk here.

The bats, by the way, are not doing well, here in the heart of bat country. Thirty years of chemical agriculture and DDT are taking their predictable percentage. According to Park Service naturalists, the bats are succumbing to the effects of pesticides in this manner: the adult bats consume the poisoned insect life but continue to live and reproduce. Their young, however, though born alive, suffer with high frequency an inability to cling to the ceilings of caves, apparently because of calcium deficiency in their claws. Unable to attach themselves to the stone alongside their mothers, the newborn fall to the cavern floors. There they die, not from the fall, but from starvation; a mother bat will not attempt to recover or suckle any of her young who leave her side.

Because of this higher rate of infant mortality, the total bat population goes into decline. As the bat population declines, the insect population, natural prey of the bats, increases in surrounding areas. (A bat will eat several times its own weight in insects each night of the active season.) As the insect population increases, the farmers apply heavier doses of insecticides and pesticides to their fields, thus poisoning more bats, and creating through natural selection a stronger, meaner race of bugs.

The great clouds of bats that once issued every day at twilight from the mouth of Carlsbad Caverns and other cave systems in the Guadalupe Mountain area are not seen anymore. The clouds have been reduced to swarms, the swarms to flights. The bats will be missed, especially by farmers, unless, with the current ban on DDT, the bats are able to regain their former numbers. If it is not already too late.

The Guadalupe Mountains are the exposed portion of an ancient coral barrier reef, most of the reef now buried beneath the desert plain of West Texas. Shaped like a giant horseshoe, the reef extends from the Guadalupes northeast into New Mexico (including Carlsbad Caverns), curves east and south back into Texas, rises again above the surface in what are called the Glass Mountains near the town of Alpine and terminates in the uplifted Apache Mountains at Van Horn, Texas.

Between the presently elevated ends of this great geological structure there once flowed, in the Permian period 225 to 280 million years ago, an arm of the sea. At that time, according to geologists, the Capitan Reef (as the whole structure is called) was created and built up by the lime-secreting growth of algae and other small organisms. Later the sea disappeared, the climate changed, and the whole region was lifted several thousand feet by underlying crustal movements of the earth. Through the millennia that followed, the higher portions of the reef, formed of harder stuff than the surrounding terrain, were gradually exposed by surface erosion. The highest point of the ancient reef, Guadalupe Peak, is now a mile above the low-lying salt beds on the west and southwest.

As would be expected, the limestone Guadalupe Mountains contain many caves and caverns, some of them possibly connected to unexplored branches of Carlsbad Caverns. But the caves of Guadalupe are not open to the public. Again, park regulations spell it out: "Caves. Entry is not permitted into any cave without written permission of the superintendent. Permission will be granted only to qualified speleologists engaged in investigations which have demonstrable value to the National Park Service in its management and understanding of the park."

Clear enough. But the reason—"safety"—is not clear. When did we grant the Park Service the right to protect us from ourselves? Surely any freeborn citizen, qualified or not, has a perfect license to risk his or her fool neck by groping downward through musty darkness into the entrails of the mountain—this mountain or any mountain.

Not that it matters much to most people. There is ample wilderness at Guadalupe National Park on the surface of things—77,500 acres of it. Guadalupe has fifty-five miles of primitive trails but little in the way of roads. U.S. Highway 62/180 passes through the southeast corner of the park for six miles; a few old-time wagon roads, too rocky and high centered for modern automobiles, approach the eastern canyons and wind across the desert *bajadas* (alluvial slopes) on the west side. There are no other roads.

The Park Service does have tentative plans to build an elevator or tramway up the face of El Capitan, so that visitors can reach the rim without physical, mental or spiritual effort. But such frills are not needed. The climb by foot trail is difficult but not beyond the ability of any two-legged American, aged eight to eighty, in normal health.

The wind continues to blow, unceasing, unrelenting. When I asked a local woman about the wind she said that it always blows in West Texas, always—from January to December. Must be hard to get used to, I suggested. We never get used to it, she said; we just put up with it.

The sun is dropping into a mass of clouds on the west. Time to get off this overexposed peak. We pick our way down the deer path of a trail, into the twilight of the canyon, toward our camp. The rugged, naked walls of El Capitan, stem of the range, loom above us on the left, cutting off our view of the sunset. We grope through a jungle of scrub pine and scrub oak, prickly pear, sawtooth sotol and rasp-edged bear grass, to the smoked cof-feepot, blackened skillet, bread and wine and meat and beans of camp, home for the night.

Next day, with loaded packs and the morning sun on our shoulders, we climb the rough switchbacks of Bear Canyon Trail. Our starting point is a place known locally as the Pinery, once a stage stop on the route of the Butterfield Overland Mail, one of the few places in this area with reliable, potable water. My wife and I carry five gallons of water, two for her, three for me—forty pounds—an unpleasant burden but necessary. We are planning a two- or three-day hike up to the rim of the main range, across the interior and down into McKittrick Canyon in the northeast quarter of the park, and from there out to the highway—a total distance of about twenty-five miles. We carry so much water because we've been assured that no more water is likely to be found until we descend McKittrick Canyon, with its permanent spring-fed stream.

The climb to the rim, two thousand feet up in little more than a mile, on a trail consisting mostly of cactus and loose stones resting at unstable angles of repose, takes us four hours. Of those four hours, two are spent in rest and watering stops. But again, it is worth it, as step-by-step we leave the desert heat behind, lessen our load of water, and reach finally the shade of the first ponderosa pine.

The change from sun-beaten rocky slope to shady, pine-fragrant forest is abrupt, startling and welcome. We rest for a while in the shade, then follow the little-used and primitive trail into the woods, going down into the area called "the Bowl." This part of the Guadalupe Range is well forested despite the absence of surface water; rainfall tends to percolate through the limestone to emerge in the canyon bottoms below. We walk under yellow pine, white fir and limber pine, through occasional glades of aspen, and, in moister places, a few Douglas firs.

This is a relict forest, a holdover from the much more extensive forests of the Pleistocene epoch, when, after the recession of the continental ice sheets, a cooler and wetter climate prevailed here. The aspens are of special interest; with the single exception of some scrawny cousins in the Chisos Mountains of Texas's Big Bend National Park, this is the southernmost group of *Populus tremuloides* in the entire United States.

Hidden among these Pleistocene trees are remnants of Pleistocene wildlife. Somewhere up here, scattered in small bands, is a herd of about 185 elk. A native animal, the elk was exterminated by early settlers in the area, then reintroduced as a herd of 44 in 1926. Though not so abundant as the mule deer, the elk are often seen by visitors to the canyons and by hikers on the ridges. The animals range in small and scattered bands because of the scarcity of water.

It must be a pleasant experience, I'm thinking, to stand on the west escarpment of the Gaudalupes in autumn, gazing out over the salt desert immediately below, and hear a bull elk trumpet his mating call from the woods around Bush Mountain or Lost Peak or Upper Dog Canyon or the Devil's Hell. A sort of faunal unconformity, it might seem. The Guadalupe Range is truly a biotic island in the desert sea.

Where there are deer and elk there should be lion, but the lion—mountain lion, I mean, *Felis concolor*—is as scarce here as most everywhere else. Not because of lack of game but from lack of room: Guadalupe Mountains National Park is too small to protect mountain lions: 77,500 acres is not enough. The lions tend to range beyond park boundaries into the surrounding ranch lands, getting themselves into deep trouble with local cattle growers, a vocational group notoriously intolerant of any predators but themselves.

Black bear and bighorn sheep were once numerous here but are now rarely seen. Like the mountain lion, the bear needs ample room to prevent his activities from interfering with those of humans. This park is not big enough for bear either. Only the bighorn sheep might do well in the Guadalupes if reintroduced. The problem for the Park Service is to find a surplus of bighorns somewhere (there is none) and to obtain the funds necessary to finance transplanting, if some could be found. The transplantation of bighorn sheep is a difficult, delicate and expensive operation—about fifteen thousand dollars per animal at present costs.

We camp our first night in the middle of somewhere—we aren't sure where, having lost the trail. But it's a good place, a grassy clearing near the trees. We build no fire—none needed—and eat with satisfaction our cold supper of nuts, cheese, jerky and fruit. It is water, more than anything else, which we think about. We have drunk so much, climbing up the trail through the heat, that we have only two gallons left. But that should be enough to get us to McKittrick Canyon the next day.

In the morning, aided by a topographical map, we find our way back to the trail, such as it is, and continue through the Bowl and up out of the pines to McKittrick Ridge. Here the trail is easier to follow, since it is not interbraided with deer paths. The views from this high ridge are spectacular, and we spend most of the day enjoying them, reluctant—except for concern over our dwindling water supply—to return to the lowlands. We camp the second night at an "official designated campsite" on the rim of McKittrick Canyon, near the beginning of the descent. The place looks attractive and seldom used; it is out of the wind, with a spacious view to the east.

In the morning, out of water, we start down the trail. This operation turns out to be nearly as arduous as the climb two days before: a two-thousand-foot descent over loose stone and gravel, down a series of switchbacks. But our loads are much lighter, gravity is with us, not against us, and we can see, far below, the glittering limestone bedrock of the stream bed and the sparkle of running water.

When at last we get there, the water tastes as good as it had looked from above. All downgrade from here on. Bellies full and gurgling, we stroll at an easy pace down the canyon, under the shade of giant cottonwoods, sycamores and wild walnut trees. The canyon seems full of birds—seventy different species have been identified here—and deer sign is everywhere. If before we had been on an island in the desert, we are now in a desert oasis.

McKittrick Canyon is home for many plants from several different environments. Here the Chihuahuan Desert interpenetrates the pine-oak forest, the easternmost mountains of the basin-and-range province meet the short-grass prairie of the high plains, and the northern extremity of Mexico's Sierra Madre touches the southern extremity of the Rocky Mountains. The result is a pleasing variety of unusual floral associations: ponderosa pine and the century plant; the sotol growing next to a Douglas fir; creosote bush side by side with bigtooth maple; chokeberry and Torrey yucca; willow trees and Englemann prickly pear; pinyon pine, one-seed juniper and maidenhair fern; Gambel oak; the hop hornbeam, and the treelike shrub known as Texas madrona.

At first glance the madrona looks a little like an overgrown manzanita, to which it might be related. But the madrona grows straighter, taller, and the bark is a different color, not mahogany red like the manzanita but a subtle blend of gray, lavender and pink. Some of the madronas are protected from hungry deer by Park Service enclosures of rabbit wire eight feet high. Out of place in a wilderness preserve, you might think, but apparently necessary to protect the madronas from the deer. The story is a familiar one: not enough mountain lions, too many deer, constant hunger, potential famine.

Sooner or later the Park Service here is going to have to deal with the politically touchy problem of how to dispose of the surplus deer—allow temporary hunting by sportsmen (recreational gunners) or have the rangers do it. The first choice would violate National Park precedent and purpose and arouse the wrath of conservationists; the second would outrage sportsmen. The proper solution—to expand the park boundaries and encourage the return of the mountain lion—would enrage the locals and maybe drive the state of Texas right out of the Union. The familiar story: too many people in a shrinking world, not enough man-eating predators.

We come to an old stone house at a fork in the canyon. This house, a certified historic site, was built in the 1920s by a wealthy petroleum geologist named Wallace E. Pratt, the same whose family later donated to the nation much of the land that forms the core of Guadalupe Mountains National Park. The house lies two miles beyond the end of the public road but is being used and maintained by the Park Service. Inside we find a pair of student naturalists banding live bats, part of an ongoing biotic inventory. These are the first fellow humans we've seen in three days. We easily persuade one of them—a young woman—to join us on the walk to the roadhead, where she gives us a ride in her car back to our own base at Pine Spring Canyon, twelve miles away. On the drive she tells us about the bats and their current problem. Like most wildlife biologists, she has little sympathy for the human animal and *its* current problems, most of which, in her opinion, are self-created and self-inflicted.

On our final two days at Guadalupe we drive seven miles of winding jeep road to the abandoned Williams ranch house under the grand west-facing escarpment of the Capitan Reef. The old house sits at the mouth of a defile called Bone Canyon. Below are the miles of dry salt basins (sometimes covered with water); above us sedimentary foothills rise to the great cliffs, a frankly vertical, perhaps unscalable, limestone wall.

The house is a one-story stud-frame shack with windows boarded over, its sides creaking in the wind, cracking apart splinter by splinter under the sun. We investigate the disintegrating corral, the rabbit hutch, the chicken house, a rusted water tank, the remains of a flatbed wagon with oaken tongue and iron-rimmed wooden-spoked wheels. Relics from the 1920s and 1930s.

Standing here amid this dereliction, one contemplates (maybe recalls) that former style of life. Many miles by dirt road to the nearest town. Saturday afternoon at the moving picture show. Return by starlight to the homestead. Unharnessing the team, forking hay into the manger, milking the cow. Inside the shack, Maw trims the wick of the kerosene lamp.

Survival chores. A hard life? No doubt. But, speaking as one whose boyhood was spent in a similar kind of life, I can think of worse things. Spending your days monitoring a computer, for example, inside the air-conditioned fluorescent-lighted womb of some glass-walled data center over in Houston, Tucson or Moscow. With windows that don't open and ranks of fellow robots all wearing dark neckties and white shirts. That would be intolerably worse.

We climb into Bone Canyon, so-named not for recent skeletons but for fossil souvenirs of the Permian period, 250 million years ago. Deep time—how easily the incomprehensible numbers roll off the mind. Geological fantasies, I sometimes think. But right here beneath my hand, embedded in the dogmatic, empirical rock, lie the petrified images of trilobites, brachiopods, crinoids. I can touch and caress them with my fingers. They exist. Whatever that means. Could the paleontologists be correct?

A rusted waterline, twisted and broken by flash floods, leads to a small spring high in the canyon. We follow the mangled pipe to the water. Two elephantine cottonwood trees stand by the spring, their gay green leaves shaking in the breeze. We fill our canteens from the trickle in the rock. Not much of an oasis, but the water tastes potable. We drink it with gratitude.

Afterward, for a long time, we sit in the shade of the blessed trees, listening to canyon wrens, to the scream of a red-tailed hawk high against the cliffs, to the moan of the wind. We watch the evening sun go down beyond the dry lakes of salt and the far northwestern mountains out in New Mexico. This is a harsh, dry, bitter place, lonely as a dream. But I like it. I know that I could live here if I wanted to. If I had to. After all, I've been here before.

EIGHT

DOWN TO THE SEA
OF CORTEZ

 From the terrace of my old stone house in the Santa Catalina foothills, we've been circling outward, farther and farther from the crowded haunts of Americans, into the wilderness. Each expedition took us a little greater distance from the cities and from what Thomas Wolfe called "the manswarm." Now we come to where the desert meets the Sea of Cortez. This is the wildest, least developed part of Mexico, and therefore the best. I invited my friend and neighbor Richard Felger to join me for a trip down there.

He is a botanist who has specialized in the ethnobotany—people and plants—of northwestern Sonora. We made our preparations and one January day got off to an early start at the crack of noon—early for us, anyhow—and headed south for the border. Avoiding the slow-moving entry at the city of Nogales, we took a little-traveled dirt road farther to the west and entered Mexico by way of the village of Sasabe, barely detectable on the maps, which is one of the nicer things about it.

ALTO, says the road sign by the Mexican border station. We halted, entered the station, obtained our tourist cards and tipped the inspector the customary dollar's worth of pesos. Leaving, I savored those smells characteristic of Mexico—refried beans, burning lard, mesquite and ironwood smoke, stale beer, manure, hot sheet iron, old adobe baking under the heat of the desert sun. It seemed good to be back.

We drove south by southwest over a rough, rocky, winding dirt road, past mile after mile of burnt adobe brickworks (apparently the chief local industry, after cattle raising), and then into the open desert. Buzzards circled overhead—there always seem to be more buzzards in the sky on the Mexican side of the border. Why? Because both life and death are more abundant down in Mexico. It's the kind of country buzzards love. A candid country, harsh and bare, which is no doubt why it strikes us overcivilized Americans as crude, vulgar and dangerous.

Scrub cattle ranging through the bush galloped off like gnus and wildebeests at our approach. I never saw such weird, scrawny, pied, mottled, humped, long-horned and camel-necked brutes trying to pass as domestic livestock. Most looked like a genetic hash of Hereford, Charolais, Brahman, Angus, moose, ibex, tapir and nightmare. Weaned on cactus, snakeweed and thistle, they showed the gleam of the sun through the translucent barrel of their rib cages. But they could run, they were alive—not only alive but vigorous. I was tempted to think, watching their angular hind ends jouncing away through the dust, that the meat on those critters, if you could find any, might just taste better than the aerated, water-injected, hormone-inflated beef we Americans get from today's semiautomated feedlots in the States.

For most of the afternoon we rambled toward the setting sun through the rolling desert of mesquite, creosote, paloverde and cactus. The saguaros were sparse and stunted looking; even the prickly pear and cholla do not seem to do well down here. But the mesquite thrives, growing in dwarf forests over what used to be grassy savanna according to ecohistorians (overgrazing—the old story). Every now and then we'd descend into a wash or arroyo where the vegetation was denser and more varied. Here Felger would stop to beat through the brush, searching for various shrubs and annuals. Some people collect stamps or beer bottles or wagon wheels; professional botanists collect weeds, press them between wooden plates, and store them away in museum files never to be seen by light of day again.

In the evening we paused for an hour to cook our supper on a heap of incandescent ironwood coals. Coyotes wailed the sun down; heavy-footed cattle stumbled through the chaparral; somebody turned on a few stars. We were down in the Mexican desert and pretty pleased with ourselves; it seemed like a retreat through time—of about fifty years. The night was long and chilly. We were glad to be heading south when the blue dawn arrived.

🖎

Into the backlands, the back of beyond, the original and primitive Mexico. For the next three days we would see few human beings and not a motor vehicle of any kind, nor a gas station, nor a telephone pole. The inevitable vultures soaring overhead reminded us, though, that somewhere in this brushy wilderness was life, sentient creation, living meat. Hard to see, of course, during the day, for most desert animals keep themselves concealed in the bush or in burrows under the surface of the ground. But you could see their tracks: birds, lizards, rodents, now and then a coyote, here and there the handlike footprints of raccoon, the long claws of badger, the prints of ring-tailed cat, the heart-shaped hoof marks of deer and javelina, the rounded pads of bob-cat, the long narrow tracks of the coatimundi, or *chulu*, as the Mexicans call it.

I have barely begun to name the immense variety of mammals, large and small, that inhabit this area. There are, for example, dozens of species of little rodents—rock squirrels, pocket go-phers, pocket mice, grasshopper mice, cactus mice, kangaroo rats, wood rats, prairie dogs—and a large assortment of skunks, cottontail rabbits, jackrabbits, porcupines, kit foxes and gray foxes.

Some of these animals, especially the rodents and other smaller mammals, may never drink free water in their entire lives. Instead they get by on what moisture they can obtain from plant food and through the internal manufacture of what is called "metabolic water." Particularly distinguished in this regard is the kangaroo rat, which subsists on a diet of dried seeds, bathes itself in sand, ignores green and succulent plants, and shuns water even when it is available.

But of all these Sonoran beasts surely the most curious is *Nasua narica*, the chulu, or coatimundi. Generally chulus travel in bands of a dozen or more, sometimes as many as two hundred, according to report. But the first one I ever saw was a loner—the older males are often solitary—prowling in a garbage dump near the town of Nogales. Preoccupied with its search for something to eat, the chulu ignored me, or perhaps did not perceive me, and I had ample opportunity to observe it closely.

It was an old one, a grandfather no doubt, unable to keep up with its band, which would also explain why it had been reduced to scavenging in a dump for survival. It was about four feet long, including the two-foot tail, which in the chulu is held upright, at a right angle to the body. The fur was rusty brown, the tail marked with light and dark rings like that of a raccoon, which the chulu somewhat resembles. But it looked a little like a small bear, too, with long hind legs and shambling gait. In fact it looked like a mixture of several mammals, with the tail of a raccoon, the gait of a bear, the nose of a pig, a face masked like that of a badger, long wolflike canine teeth and the lean slab-sided body of a fox or coyote.

As I watched this chulu, I saw it turn over rocks, tin cans, boards and other junk with its front paws, exhibiting the manual dexterity of a human. It was probably searching for insects, grubs, arachnids and snakes, as it spent a great deal of time rooting about underneath things with its long and flexible snout. I have learned since that chulus, like coyotes and javelinas, will eat most anything they can find or catch; like us, they are omnivorous.

To see what it would do, I walked toward the chulu, whistled and held out one hand. It looked at me with soft brown eyes, seemingly full of trust, but a snarling grin that exposed long yellow fangs conveyed a different impression. I would not have cared to tangle with this animal bare-handed, but before I got close enough to risk attack it turned tail and scurried as nimbly as a tomcat up the trunk of a big juniper.

My favorite desert animal, I think, after such obvious choices as coyote, vulture, cougar, ring-tailed cat, Gila monster and gopher snake, is the whimsical, cockeyed, half-mad, always eccentric, more or less lovable *Pecari angulatus sonoriensis*, otherwise known as javelina or peccary. A herd of them scampered across the road in front of us as we bounced over the backlands toward the sea. We stopped and watched them go up a hillside and over the crest, the dust flying from their busy hoofs.

What are javelinas? Well, they are piglike animals, but they are not true pigs. They look more like razorback hogs, but they are not true razorbacks either. Someone has likened them to a child's notion of what a pig should look like. They are comical, myopic, vicious and excitable. They have sharp little hoofs, pointed ears, small square bodies and huge heads mounted on massive necks; neck and head appear to take up nearly half the total body volume. The tail is so small as to be ridiculous, but the teeth are sharp. Javelinas are capable (it is said) of inflicting severe—even fatal—damage upon anyone unlucky enough to find himself between a charging javelina and an immovable wall.

I remembered my first encounter with javelinas. I was blundering about in the Sonoran hills, daydreaming as usual, when I gradually became aware of a snorting, snuffling sound ahead, accompanied by the shuffle of many active hoofs. The terrain was brushy, the lilac twilight falling about me, so that I could not see much, and besides I was listening primarily to the melancholy chorus of red-spotted toads in the canyon below. I crashed on through the thickets. The nearsighted javelinas did not notice my approach until I almost stumbled over them. At that point the herd exploded in all directions at once, two of them stampeding past me so close on either side that I felt the friction of their bristles. They must have been even more startled than I was. A moment later I stood alone in a now-quiet clearing, among uprooted roots and overturned stones, and sniffed at the curious musky odor in the air. Off in the distance, at sixteen different compass points, I could still hear the panicked scramble, the outraged snorts, squeals and grunts, of the shattered herd of javelinas. It must have taken them hours to get properly reassembled and back to their evening feed.

As with humans and chulus, javelinas will eat anything—snails, locusts, roots, berries, clams, truffles, mushrooms, garlic, bugs, birds, eggs, general assorted garbage. This is reputed to be an indication of intelligence. Living in the Sonoran Desert, however, the javelina specializes in the consumption of cactus—

spines, barbs, hooks, needles, thorns, hair and all; its favorite cactus is the succulent pad of the prickly pear.

The javelina also fancies the barrel cactus—that bloated monster of a vegetable that rises up like an overgrown green fireplug, leaning south over the sunny sides of hills. But the barrel cactus, armored by an intricate network of rosy claws, cannot easily be approached, except for the yellowish fruit on top, which the javelina and other creatures will extricate and consume in due season. The only way a javelina can get at the tender insides of a barrel cactus is from the base, which is sometimes exposed when excessive growth or a storm or a weakened root system causes the plant to keel over. Then the javelina, seizing its chance, drops to its knees and burrows headfirst into the bottom of the now-defenseless plant. I have never actually seen this performance but I have seen barrel cactus fallen over and hollowed out, surrounded by the scuffle marks and scat of the javelina.

🐾

On to the sea. All day long Felger and I rattled through the desert; we passed a few small rancherias where mesquite-branch corrals, idle windmills and small mud huts attested to the part-time presence of our fellow men. But we saw no one. We passed other ranches obviously abandoned. Herds of starving cattle appeared from time to time but not so frequently as before.

Ahead was a cactus-studded horizon. We topped a rise and came to our first cardon, a cactus related to and resembling the Arizona saguaro, but with many more branches, greater mass, a more bronzed, massive and sculptured appearance. The older, properly aged, wind-blasted and sun-scorched cardons look as if they'd been hammered out of bronze and old iron by some demented junkyard genius from Hoboken, New Jersey. The biggest cardons grow tall as the noblest saguaros, maybe taller; they must weigh three times as much. In girth, near the base, where the mighty branches start, they could equal the biggest oak or cottonwood. Like the saguaro, the cardon is columnar in structure, with flexible fluting in trunk and branch to permit gains and losses in moisture content. Compared to the cardon the saguaro seems slender, even graceful, almost elegant; compared to the saguaro the cardon is a crude hulking brute of an organism. I'll take the cardon.

Tastes differ. I asked Dr. Felger to name his favorite vegetable. "I am a scientist," he said. "I refuse to make value judgments." Spoken like a true scientist. Then he added, "They are all my friends."

Finally we came to a pass in the desert hills. We paused to contemplate an infinite band of blue, a misty shimmer of vapor and sky that merged one with the other beyond the end of land. We were coming at last to the sea, El Mar de Cortez, or, as it is identified on most maps, the Gulf of California.

As we approached the sea the cacti began to peter out, becoming smaller, sparser. Apparently the damp sea air does not entirely agree with them. First the cardons disappeared, then the saguaros, then the others. Last to hold out, sometimes on the dunes behind the beach, were the senita and a few scrubby specimens of cholla.

The road we were following brought us to a fishing village called Puerto Libertad, inhabited by half a dozen families of Seri Indians and on occasion by American tourists and fishermen. We could see the huts of the Indians, at the northern end of the bay, and two houses built by American colonists, near the beach, but since we had no business with any of those people and needed no supplies, we turned south on a road—a single-lane sand track—paralleling the coast.

After a few miles we turned off and took a seaward trail to inspect the beach and the gulf. We found first a natural water hole or spring, within half a mile of the beach. From this water hole, lined with tules and Olney bulrushes, innumerable trails radiated in various directions, revealing the visitation of the usual scrub cattle and other desert mammals. I tasted the water: saline, but evidently not so salty that the animals would not drink it. At some point the hole or seep had been enlarged and fenced in with a few strands of barbed wire, long since broken through.

Dr. Felger found much of interest around this well—more weeds. But I was aware of something else, something I hadn't heard for a year—the clamor of the sea. It came from over the brow of the dunes, where saltbush and marsh grass shivered in the wind, gulls circled, screaming, and a lone osprey searched for its supper.

I climbed the ridge and saw the beach curving in a smooth crescent for many miles, north and south, completely deserted. A strong wind roiled the water. The glare of the sun, the glittering waves, dazzled my eyes as I loped down the dune to the shore. Felger caught up with me and we walked the strand and hunted souvenirs. We found shark eggs, sand dollars, kelp, starfish, rotting sponges, the shell of a fiddler crab. I looked inside: nobody home. We found bleach bottles, tequila bottles, tin cans, fragments of boat and fishing tackle, and other jetsam, all modified by passage through the salty sea. Strange to find such garbage on this lonely shore.

The next day we took off for points still farther south. We were now entering the most varied desert garden I had ever seen. First and predominant were the great cardons, towering fifty and sixty feet. Here and there were the familiar saguaros, organ-pipes and senitas, and one new to me, what the Mexicans call *agria*, an ugly sinister reptilian thing that crawls and twists over the ground in knots. There were the many kinds of prickly pear and cholla, including Schott's cholla and the purple staghorn cholla, which conceals its chlorophyll beneath a purplish skin.

Some of the agave plants, we saw, were about ready to erect their mighty stalks and burst into the one great efflorescence of their glorious and tragic careers. Now is the time, said Dr. Felger, to eat them. When the center leaves begin to part, he explained, that is the time to dig up the agave, cut out its heart, roast the heart on slow coals and eat it. Especially delicious, he continued, when seasoned with a bit of wild garlic—and he knelt and with his fingers dug up a tiny, obscure little green plant that I had not noticed. He scraped the dirt from the white bulb at the end of the roots and offered it to me. I ate it. It was good, more like scallion than garlic.

The next day we tooled across mile-long ceramic dry lake beds, then through more of the lonely, lovely, delectable wilds, among the giant cactus, past a background panorama of jagged iron mountains. We were headed for Cape Tepoca and the bay beyond it on the south. Rounding the headland and coming toward the bay, we gained a view of Tiburón Island, itself a half-sunken mountain range surrounded by the waters of the gulf. To the north of Tiburón, I saw a small island that looked like a pyramid covered with snow. A rookery for seabirds, Felger explained; the white stuff is guano.

We left the main road and followed a dirt track that skirted mangrove estuaries, then faded out between the shore and the steep slope of the mountain. There we stopped and cooked supper beside the shingle beach. As we ate, we watched ponderous brown pelicans flap in formation above the waves, then peel off and plunge straight down into the water, like dive bombers, and come up with fish. Dolphins passed by some fifty yards offshore. An osprey sailed out from its home in the cactus forest, skimmed over the surface of the water, caught a fish and lugged it through the air back to a shaggy nest on the top of a cardon. Watching the bird through field glasses I saw it tear off and eat the fish's head: always the best part first.

For several days and nights we lounged along that shore between the desert and the sea, under the intense sun and splendid light, unknown mountains behind us, the equally unknown mountains of Baja California across the gulf. I walked for hours on the golden beach, swam in the cold clear salt water, wandered through the cactus forest. It is the kind of place where you can do absolutely nothing for days on end and only wish you could do even less.

When time came to leave, we drove down the coast road to Kino Bay, then east from Kino to Hermosillo, capital city of the state of Sonora. Back to the real world: miles of miserable human slums, miles of smoke, dust, butchered hills, scalped cotton fields and chicken factories, a part of Sonora's brand-new industrial agriculture. Mexico, too, rushes into the future.

I thought of the wilderness we had left behind us, open to sea and sky, joyous in its plenitude and simplicity, perfect yet vulnerable, unaware of what is coming, defended by nothing, guarded by no one.

NINE

THE ANCIENT DUST

The seldom seen Western American desert rat is just another poor bare forked featherless biped, like the rest of us, but he has certain peculiar features: a permanent squint, a hide well pricked with cactus acupunctures, the big toes purple and dead from kicking stones and inside the skull a sun-baked cranky semimisanthropic brain. And he's happy.

The desert rat loves water but prefers to live, like his four-footed cousin the kangaroo rat, where water is rare as radium. The rarity makes it precious, therefore lovable. For this rat the finest of all music is the tinkle of seep water trickling into a tin cup, the periodic drip of unseen water drops falling in the shadows upon tympanic stone.

He is tolerably adapted to intense heat, constant glare, sand in his eggs, scorpions in his shoes, kissing bugs in his bedroll. He doesn't mind a landscape composed mostly of naked rock with some scrubby-looking plants creeping cautiously out of the cracks; in fact he tends to find green pastures and grassy lawns claustrophobic. Which brings us to space, outer-inner space, and the desert rat's special fetishes.

He loves all forms of life, even people. But though he loves people (in moderation), he prefers to see them, like trees and bushes, spaced well apart. At a comfortable spitting distance from one another—say, two miles—with a sawtooth hogback monocline about five hundred feet high in between for a fence.

This is not meant to suggest that the desert rat is necessarily tougher than other rats. He is certainly not nearly so tough, for example, as the *Rattus rattus urbanus*, that highly specialized breed that thrives or at least survives on cement and steel, clamor and crime, gasoline fumes and the deadly double dry martini. Compared to him the desert rat is a dainty, fastidious epicene, tender as a water lily. But the desert rat carries one distinction like a halo: he has learned to love the kind of country that most people find unlovable. Call the desert barren, harsh, bitter, dreary and gloomy, acrid and arid, lifeless, hopeless, ugly as sin, ghastly as the gates of hell—he will happily agree with you. Because in his heart lies the secret belief that the awful desert is really sweet and lovable, that the ugly is really beautiful, that hell is home. And if others think he's crazy, so much the better; he is reluctant to share his love anyway.

Even for desert rats, however, there are limits. Some think that the bloodsucking cone-nosed kissing bug is too much of a good thing. Some draw the line at centipedes that drop from the ceiling into your fried eggs. Some hesitate at six-foot diamondbacks coiled on the welcome mat in the evening. But these are petty annoyances. More serious divisions of opinion between desert rats concern places. Some, for example, feel that Death Valley, in the summertime, at 130 degrees Fahrenheit in the shade, is going too far. Most would agree, however, that the ultimate among the various provinces of the Great American Desert is Sonora's Pinacate region, at the head of the Gulf of California. This is the bleakest, flattest, hottest, grittiest, grimmest, dreariest, ugliest, most useless, most senseless desert of them all. It is the villain among badlands, most wasted of wastelands, most foreboding of forbidden realms. At least in the Southwest, the Pinacate Desert is the final test of desert rathood; it is here that we learn who is a true rat and who essentially is only a grasshopper mouse.

One cannot claim that Pinacate is a scenic area in any common sense of the word. The deserts of northern Arizona and southern Utah feature sheer-walled canyons thousands of feet deep, entrenched for five hundred miles through great plateaus; the biggest "canyon" in Pinacate is a gulch about 40 feet deep and ten miles long. Almost anywhere else in the Southwest you will see real mountains at least somewhere on the horizon, with snow fields and alpine flora; but in Pinacate country the highest point is Pinacate Peak itself, a tired old dome-shaped volcano (extinct) rising only 3,957 feet above sea level. Hardly enough elevation to cast a shadow or float a cloud. Volcanic phenomena are a Pinacate specialty, but even in this aspect its cinder cones, craters and lava flows do not equal in color and dramatic form those of the Sunset Crater region of northern Arizona.

Well then, you ask, what *is* the attraction? Why should anyone go out of his way to contemplate the Pinacate country, El Gran Desierto, this ultimate wasteland?

One answer might be that very few people ever do go out there. A few Mexican woodcutters; a few hardened hot-country fanatics from the States. But this is not an answer, only an evasion. Perhaps the explanation is that the appeal of the Pinacate country lies in its total lack of any obvious appeal. In its emptiness. In its vast, desolate nothingness. At its heart is a 750-square-mile volcanic field, an iron-hard, iron-hued wilderness of craters, cones, congealed lava flows, with Pinacate Peak in the middle. To the south lie the empty salt marshes, the sandy hummocks that border the coast of the Sea of Cortez. On the north and east are rugged little granite ranges and more cactus and creosote desert, inhabited by starving cattle and other wild animals. On the outskirts of this desert are the towns of Sonoita, San Luisito and Puerto Peñasco, with a combined population of maybe sixty thousand people. Which isn't much for an area the size of Pennsylvania.

And then there is the erg.

The erg is a sea of sand, an ocean of dunes stretching from the base of Pinacate Peak on its west side to what is left of the Colorado River and its now-lifeless delta at the head of the gulf. From peak to delta is a distance of about a hundred miles by line of sight, interrupted by a few small, isolated, waterless desert mountains. In all of the region there is nothing that can be called man-made except the highway skirting its northern edge and on the south the single railway line that runs along the coast from Mexicali to Puerto Peñasco.

The sand dunes, like the volcanic field and the glittering sea that form much of the horizon here, have one quality more overwhelming than any other: a great brooding solemnity, compounded in equal parts of distance, space, emptiness and silence. "Nothing is more real than nothing," wrote Samuel Beckett, thinking of the human soul; he could have said it of Pinacate. Thomas Hardy, too, would have found something familiar in this moorland among deserts.

"There's something about the desert," a friend once said to me, trying to explain why he loved the desert. Rather, why he loved it so *much*. And try though he would, he could say no more. I have often wondered what the answer would have been from one of the most famous of Death Valley old-timers, a prospector named Seldom Seen Slim. But he never answered his telephone. He didn't have a telephone. And he was never home. Didn't have a home.

I have tried to analyze my own emotions on this subject: why am I so much in love with the desert? I love also the sea and the seashore, the mountains, lakes and glaciers, the soft blue-green hills of my Appalachian boyhood, the plains of Oklahoma, the blue grottoes of Capri, the dark forests of Bavaria, the misty golden hills of Scotland, yes, even the back alleys of Hoboken, New York City, Berlin, Naples, Barcelona, Brisbane, Pittsburgh. There's beauty, heartbreaking beauty, everywhere. But when I think of where I want most to be, finally, it's the old hot dusty eyeball-searing head-aching skin-blistering throat-parching boot-burning bloody goddamned desert again. Why?

"There's something about the desert . . ." my friend had said. And paused. And halted. And could say no more. He might of course have mentioned the obvious things: the bracing aridity of the air, the clarity of the light (where industry has not yet shoved its brutal snout into the hinterlands), the elegant neoclassic simplicity of the landscape and landforms, the relative scarcity of man and his works, the queerness of the plant life, the admirable hardiness of the animal life, the splendor of sundown after an August storm, the rare oracular miracle of dripping springs in a nearly waterless land, the human history—the Indians fighting against cruel and hopeless odds, the Euro-American whites driving onward the frontiers of empire. All of this is true enough, but every other particular region, anywhere on earth, has its distinctive features too.

Yet none quite fulfills the peculiar appeal that the desert scene has for some of us. There is something more in the desert, something that has no name. I might call it a mystery—or simply Mystery itself, with an emphatically capital *M*. Unlike forest or seashore, mountain or city, plain or swamp, the desert, any desert, suggests always the promise of something unforeseeable, unknown but desirable, waiting around the next turn in the canyon wall, over the next ridge or mesa, somewhere within the wrinkled hills. What, exactly? Well . . . a sort of treasure. A kind of delight. God? Perhaps. Gold? Maybe. Grace? Possibly. But something a little more, a little different, even from these.

So there you are. The secret revealed, the essence uncovered, we come right back to where we started. The desert rat loves the desert because there is something about it that he cannot explain or even name.

Which brings us full wobbly circle back to Pinacate, because here is the secret allure of the desert in its purest form—simply because there is so little to compete with it: no great canyons, no mighty mountains, no spectacular flora or fauna, no weird and colorful rock formations, no winy spirits in the air. Only the bleak and brooding badlands, the shimmering sea of sand, the watery rim of the salt sea.

After the generalizations come the qualifications. As I've noted, the plant life in the Pinacate country is sparse. But the first time I visited this area was in March of 1968, a great year for desert wildflowers; the winter rains had come in just the right amounts and at proper intervals. Guided by ranger-naturalist Bill Hoy of Organ Pipe Cactus National Monument, our party approached from the east, off the Puerto Peñasco road, and drove to the end of a woodcutters' truck road at a waterless dead end called Paloverde Camp. Except for the lone paloverde that gave the place its name, there was a dearth of shade as well as water; even in March the daytime temperature was in the high eighties.

But this mattered little. What we saw, looking up from that forlorn spot among the rocks, was the two-thousand-foot-high slope of a cindery mountain all covered with a rash, a fuzzy golden coat, of blooming brittlebush, yellow flowers spread across a panorama twenty miles wide. Proceeding on foot, we found other early spring flowers in bloom: the pinkish fairy duster, the golden Mexican poppy, the scarlet-flowered hummingbird's trumpet bush and the coral-colored globe mallow. Masses of bloom. Drunken honeybees, sick with joy, zigzagged crazily from bush to bush, flower to flower, having the time of their lives.

🌠

That was the day Bill Hoy rappelled down into the well-like opening of a sixty-foot fumarole in the heart of a lava flow and nearly never emerged. We watched him go down—his Argentine wife, Marina, a friend, myself—and saw him fade into the gloom at the bottom of the pit. He poked around for a while in the ancient dust, hoping to find Indian artifacts, the pelvic bones of sacrificial virgins, a further opening to the underworld, anything novel, literary, scientific. There was nothing but darkness and dust.

He started back up the rope, pulling himself upward and out with the aid of a pair of jumars—clamplike metal devices that grip a rope with many times the leverage of human hands. This particular fumarole, however, has a pronounced overhang on its inside rim. When Bill reached it he found himself hung up. His weight pulled the rope tight against the face of the overhang so that he couldn't move the clamps up the line. He was dangling, and could not claw his way around the overhang. Nor could we risk pulling him from the top by the upper end of the rope, even though it was firmly attached to a tree near the rim of the fumarole. Bill's weight on the rope, its friction on the rock and the added strain of our tugging from above might have broken the line. The only thing we could do was lower a second line. Long, sweaty, hard-breathing minutes followed, while Bill succeeded—one-handed—in securing it around his chest. We had him belayed. Then we pulled him away from the overhang, so that he was able to use his jumars and clamber over the lip of rock. From the nettle, safety . . .

Next day we visited Crater Elegante, the deepest of Pinacate's *collapse calderas* (to use the precise geological term) formed by the sinking of subsurface magma. The result in the case of this caldera is a circular depression over a mile in diameter and approximately 850 feet deep: The walls slope at a moderate grade, so that it is possible to scramble to the bottom. Here you find a sparse growth of typical Sonoran Desert shrubbery—creosote bush and cactus—and a small population of mice and lizards and birds. There is no permanent water in Crater Elegante; the inhabitants therefore must manufacture their own water, metabolically, or obtain it from the blood and tissue of their occasional prey.

We left the volcanic field by a northerly route, skirting the frontal edge of a lava flow fifty feet high and several miles long. Here too the brittlebush was in massed bloom, and under the flowers we glimpsed the collared lizard, the leopard lizard and the fat chuckwalla, once much prized by Papago Indians as food. A fierce-looking lizard a foot long, the chuckwalla when threatened will crawl into a rock crevice and inflate itself, wedging its body tightly in place. This helps as defense against hawks and coyotes but not against hungry Indians. The Papago would deflate the lizard with a knife or sharpened stick and drag it out, squirming, to meet its fate. Which was not good, from the chuckwalla's point of view: it would be boiled alive, like a lobster, or eaten raw.

Among the Indians and Mexicans the Pinacate Desert is considered a *mal país*, an "evil land," a place better to be avoided. There is something in the landscape, the iron hills and brooding sky, the scarcity of even the simplest forms of life, that suggests magic to a certain cast of mind, thoughts of the supernatural and the occult. It's the kind of country witch doctors would like.

I found myself thinking about this on our second trip to the Pinacate country, a year after the first, in the awful heat of May. We came down from Los Vidrios on the north for a look at the western side of the desert, and on the way we stopped near what appeared to be no more than a modest rise. We climbed it and found ourselves peering down into a pit of jagged black basalt 650 feet deep: Sykes Crater. Much deeper than wide, this crater makes a more vivid impression on the senses than the accessible expanse of Crater Elegante. Here at Sykes the precipitous walls, the pitlike proportions, the angular exposure of the rock, the shadowy depths, combine to evoke the real breath and smell of the underworld.

From Sykes Crater, we drove southward for some twenty miles and three hours over the roughest, rockiest jeep trail this side of Baja California. We reached the dead end of the trail at a place called Tule Tank, where we made camp for several days and nights.

Tule Tank isn't much to look at, merely a bench of lava rock with some scrubby paloverde and saguaro, low buttes and ridges forming the horizon, but in the gulch close by is one of the few water-holding *tinajas* in the entire region, a deep tight basin in the basalt bedrock. Filled by thunderstorms and flash floods, this *tinaja* almost always contains some water. There is no other water within fifty miles.

A few words on water-hole etiquette: it is considered bad form to bathe in *tinajas*, especially by the next person who comes along needing a drink.

Once comfortably set up in the shade, what there was of it, with a couple of canvas bags of water hanging, cooling and evaporating in the hot breeze, we began to think about climbing Pinacate Peak. We thought about it all day long, reclining in the shade with our bird books and lizard books, waiting for the sun to decline to a bearable angle. In the evening we went for a long walk over the flats and thought about it some more. Off in the west, paralleling the rim of the sea, the rippled erg glimmered with light and heat, endless, depthless. We strolled across the desert pavement, under a fat rising moon, and thought about the mountain.

Desert pavement is aptly named. Very small volcanic stones and cinders, worn smooth as tile by millennia of weathering and closely packed in a matrix of silt, form a regular, level surface where few plants gain a foothold. Chemical reactions among soil, rock and air, continuing through the centuries, give the "pavement" a varnishlike patina. Some of these pavement areas extend for a mile, as wide as they are long.

The old moon drifted above, soft and silvery, well worn as a peon's last peso, shedding its indifferent light upon the grand desolation around us. Pinacate, the sleeping volcano, sloped upward on the east, half in moonlight, half in shadow.

A moonbird called. "Poor-will . . . poor-will . . . poorwill . . ." A relative of the Eastern whippoorwill, the moonbird or poorwill or *Phalaenoptilus nuttallii* has kept me awake for half of many a desert night. Especially when the moon is up. The only recourse is to crawl out of your sack and pitch rocks at the bird till he flutters off to haunt somebody else.

Risky, though. There's something weird about those moonbirds, most of all when heard in the emptiness of the Pinacate country. We looked again at the mountain. One way to exorcise any evil spirits here might be through direct confrontation, face to face, human to inhuman, upon the summit of their territory.

We would climb the mountain.

But first we spent a day out on the sea of dunes, out on the rolling erg. From the distance we had seen nothing but sand. But once out on it we discovered many forms and signs of life. There were mesquite trees, small and scattered but beautiful in their fresh green spring leafery; they too, like the paloverde, were in bloom, with a fragrance faint but sweet, smelling like apples. We saw saltbush, the four-winged variety, and clumps of smoke tree, that ghostly shrub. There were locoweed, sand verbena, coyote gourd and other plants I could not identify. Everywhere on the sand were the tracks of rats, mice, lizards, birds, snakes, beetles and butterflies. Butterfly tracks? Yes, I saw them alight, walk about, take off.

This we saw on the edge of the erg. As we tramped farther in, following the cornices of the great firm dunes, the plant life and with it the animal life became more and more scarce, until finally, maybe a mile into that silent oven of sand and sky and sun, we came to where there was no more life except ourselves, alien and alone.

Next day we climbed the mountain. No great climb, not even a scramble, but a long hike up the lower slopes and a ravine where we passed Tinaja Alta, the highest natural water tank in Pinacate. We noticed as we trudged by that it contained only a few inches of water. We left the ravine and began the tedious ascent of the peak itself. Hot up there; gravity dragged at our boots. Through scattered saguaros and stands of shiny teddy-bear cholla we tramped on until, three hours from Tule Tank, we reached the summit of Pinacate Peak.

There was nobody there but us mountain climbers. No gods, no spirits, no ghosts that I could see, only the wind and the brittlebush and a great deal of loose scaly rock. There seemed nothing to do but return.

We paused, however, for a survey of the world around us. Even though the air was hazy we could see for close to sixty miles in all directions. There was obvious Arizona on the north, mantled in smelter smog and progress. The state of Sonora to the east did not look much healthier. South stood the range of granitic mountains called Sierra Blanca; a friend named Larry May, an ecologist and fellow desert rat, would take me there later to show me a valley where he had measured the temperature, one day in June 1971, at 134 degrees Fahrenheit, which equals the highest reading ever recorded at Death Valley and is exceeded only by a figure of 136 degrees taken at a weather station called Aziziya in Libya. We named the place Infernal Valley.

We gazed southwest and west, beyond the craters and the cones toward the erg, which forms a golden crescent on the verge of the sea. Both the blue sea and the sea of sand extended farther than our vision, fading off into the western haze and a vague suggestion of the mountains of Baja California.

We descended, down the broken rock and unstable cinders, through the ocotillo jungles and the saguaro groves. Here and there we saw a scatter of little mahogany pellets—sure sign of bighorn sheep. But the pellets were old, brittle, dry as dust. Are there any bighorns left in this place? Larry May says there are. Even mountain lions, or at least one transient mountain lion—he saw it.

The heat became greater as we hiked down from the mountain into the waiting inferno. In the middle of the afternoon we paused for an hour's rest in the shade of an ironwood by the side of La Tinaja Alta. It seemed to us that the water in the little basin had gone down since we had seen it last, two or three hours earlier. We stared at the stagnant water, its surface coated with dove feathers and a scum of dust, and dead and living bugs, bees, flies, fleas. After the climb, our canteens were empty. We were extremely thirsty. To us, despite its surface appearance, the water looked good. We drank some and felt better.

It was also good to lie on the cool blue-gray basalt under the shade of the tough old tree—ironwoods may be as long-lived as Methuselah—and watch the bees buzzing and sipping at the water's edge. The heat and glare beyond our little sheltering bower was terrific, stunning, exhausting; the heat waves looked dense enough to float a boat on. But here in the shade we knew peace of a sort, a happy bliss, ease of limb and mind. While my companion filled his canteen, straining the insect-filled tepid water through a bandana, I watched the insouciant birds creeping and flitting through the brush. *Phainopepla nitens, Pyrrhuloxia sinuata, Pipilo fuscus*—all my desert favorites were there, stoking their furious metabolisms with bug and seed, stuffing their greedy gizzards.

We prepared to go but paused for a last look at the little water hole. Our drink and filling one canteen had plainly lowered the water level another two inches. Only a bucketful or so remained. La Tinaja Alta is a very small *tinaja* to begin with, and this was the dry season. The bees crawled over the damp rim of the basin, bedraggled and puzzled. Even the bird cries seemed forlorn.

Out in the rocks and brush somewhere crouched other small animals waiting for us to leave, waiting their turn for a drink. We didn't see them, we didn't hear them, but we felt them. We knew they were there.

Four miles to go, a good two hours' march (on that terrain) before we reached camp and the big *tinaja* of Tule Tank. We thought about the birds and bees and animals, the injustice of life, the general harshness of existence. I know, it's tough all over, but nowhere tougher than on the blackened slopes of Pinacate, under that pitiless Sonoran sun.

All the water we had was in the one canteen. We emptied it back into the little stony basin. Not in charity but out of caution. It seemed, after all, no more than a prudent sacrifice to the spirit of the desert.

TEN

GATHER AT THE RIVER

 In medias res, Alaska, June 24, 1983—We watch the little Cessna roar down the gravel bar toward the river, going away. Leaving. At full throttle, into the wind, pilot and airplane are fully committed: they must take off or die. Once again the miracle takes place: the fragile craft lifts itself from the ground and rises into the air, noisy as a bumblebee, delicate as a butterfly. Function of the airfoil, pulled forward by a whirling screw. Despite quantum mechanics and Heisenberg's uncertainty principle, planes fly.

If only by statistical probability, they continue to fly, most of the time. And I am delighted, one more time, by the daring of my species and the audacity of our flying machines. There is poetry and music in our technology, a beauty as touching as that of eagle, moss campion, raven or yonder limestone boulder shining under the Arctic sun.

The airplane diminishes downriver, banks and turns through a pass in the hills and is gone, out of sight, suddenly silent, ephemeral and lovely as a dream.

I notice now that we have been left behind. Two of us, myself and Dana Van Burgh III, a handsome, hearty young man who looks a bit like Paul McCartney or maybe one of Elvis Presley's possible sons by way of Linda or Stevie or Jesse, good sound symmetric genes interlocked in a Rubik's Cube of hereditary co-efficiency. But we're treading on a cluster of taboos here—better back off. I'm not too sure about Elvis anyway.

But we have definitely been left behind. The Cessna is bound for an Eskimo village called Kaktovik ("fish seining place") about one hundred miles away on the most dismal, desperate, degraded rathole in the world—Barter Island. If all goes well the plane will return in two hours with more of our equipment and two or three more members of our party. Our expedition. Mark Jensen's Alaska River Expeditions, Inc., Haines, Alaska.

The river at our side, more crystalline than golden, is called the Kongakut, and the plan, if all goes right, is to float down this river in two rubber rafts to another straight gravel bar eighty miles downstream. There, ten days from now, the airplane will pick us up and ferry us back to Kaktovik and Barter Island. Something to look forward to. But the river is alive with Arctic char and grayling, first-rate primeval fishing waters, and in the valley and among the treeless mountains around us roam the caribou, the wolf, the Dall sheep (close cousin to the bighorn), and of course the hypothetical grizzly bear. Himself, *Ursus arctos horribilis*. So they say.

If I seem skeptical about the bear it is because, after several efforts, I have yet to see with my own eyes a grizzly in the wild. I spent a summer as a fire lookout in Glacier National Park in Montana, saw a few black bear but not one grizzly. Even hiking alone, after dark, through alder thickets on a mountain trail, failed to attract the GRIZ. I sweated up another mountain trail behind Douglas Peacock, himself half grizzly, to a secret place he calls the Grizzly Hilton, where he has filmed, encountered, *talked with* many grizzlies, but on that one special day we saw nothing but flies, mosquitoes, and the devil's club, a mean ugly plant with hairy leaves, thorny stems, a fist of inedible yellow berries on its top. Ten days on the Tatshenshini River in the wilderness of the Yukon and southeastern Alaska again failed to produce an authentic grizzly bear. I even tried the Tucson Zoo one time, but the alleged grizzly (if such there be) refused to emerge from its den in the rear of the cage. I could see a single dark paw with ragged claws, a host of loitering flies—nothing more.

The grizzly bear is an inferential beast.

Of course I've seen the inferential evidence—the photographs and movies, the broad tracks in the sand, the deep claw marks on a spruce tree higher than I could reach, the fresh bear shit steaming like hot caviar on the trail. And I've heard and read the testimony of many others. What does it come to? Inference. If p then q. It could all be a practical joke, a hoax, even a conspiracy. Which is more likely? asked Mark Twain (I paraphrase): that the unicorn exists or that men tell lies?

The grizzly bear is a myth.

The high peaks of the Brooks Range stand behind us, to the south, barren of trees, dappled with snowfields and a few small glaciers. To the east is Canada, the border perhaps another fifty miles away. The nearest city in that direction would be Murmansk. Murmansk, Russia. The nearest city to the west is also Murmansk. The nearest city in any direction is Fairbanks, almost 400 miles to the southwest. (If you are willing to allow Fairbanks a place in the category "city." And why not? We are a generous people.) The nearest permanently inhabited or reinhabited town, after Kaktovik up there in the Beaufort Sea, is an Athapaskan Indian settlement called Arctic Village a couple of hundred miles away on the other side, the southern wetter side, of the Brooks Range. White folks, I am told, are not welcome in Arctic Village, especially after sundown. And when the sun goes down in Arctic Village it stays down, in winter, for three months.

After the Australian outback, this is the most remote spot on which I've managed to install myself on this particular planet, so far. But it seems benign here, at the moment: especially the river flowing nearby, its water clean enough to drink, directly, without boiling or purifying. Imagine the rare, almost-forgotten pleasure of dipping a cup into a river—not a stream but a river—and drinking the water at once, without hesitation, without fear. There are no beaver in the Brooks, no domestic cattle, no permanent humans and extremely few transient humans, and therefore no coliform bacteria. So far.

And the sun keeps shining, circling, shining, not so intensely as in the desert or at high elevations (we're only twenty-five hundred feet above sea level here), but more persistently. With a doughty, dogged persistence: that midsummer sun never will go down.

The breeze continues to blow from downriver, a chill wind off the ice pack ninety miles north, but welcome to us here and now because it keeps the mosquitoes busy. They cling to the brush and weeds when the wind blows, come forth for blood transfusions only when it stops. . . .

The wind stops. Instantly, like magic, the air becomes *filthy* with little black bodies, hypodermic beaks, the whine of a billion tiny flapping wings. Dana and I smear hands, necks, hair, faces with a repellent poison and set to work erecting the cook tent. The mosquitoes are annoying but tolerable; they're here for better reasons than we are. And Dana for better reasons than I: he is a professional boatman, wilderness guide, mountaineering instructor, ice climber. He is paid to be here.

We gather firewood. Timberline begins at sea level on the north side of the Brooks Range divide, but there is a scrubby growth of willow, shoulder high, along the crystal river, and little groves of small slender cottonwoods—like baby aspens—tucked in sheltered corners here and there. We garner driftwood, enough for a couple of days, from the gravel bar.

Dana stops, hearing a noise in the willow thicket downstream. A noise like a thump and thud of heavy feet. He faces that way, watching intently. The noise stops. I look the other way, upstream and to both sides, afraid of something *fierce* creeping upon us from behind.

"It ain't wilderness," says my friend Doug Peacock, "unless there's a critter out there that can kill you and eat you."

Two pump-action short-barreled shotguns lie on our duffle a hundred feet away, loaded with twelve-gauge slugs. The shotguns have two purposes: one, to frighten away an aggressive bear; two, to stop and kill a charging bear. There are no trees fit to climb on the whole North Slope. A grizzly can run thirty-five miles an hour, uphill or down, with equal facility.

Back at the Barter Island airstrip Dana had explained the shotguns in the following way to one of our passengers: "You fire the first shot in front of the GRIZ, into the ground, to scare him away. If he don't scare but keeps advancing, you wait until you can't stand it anymore, then shoot to kill. First a shot to knock him down, next a shot to finish him off."

The masculine pronoun is a mere convention. The female grizzlies are as unpredictable as the males. There is no sure way anyhow, short of an intimate body examination, for a human to identify the sexes. A female with cubs, of course, is far more dangerous than the male. The males are bigger.

I especially like Dana's phrase *until you can't stand it anymore.* Thoroughly subjective but admirably rational. How close is too close? According to Edward Hoagland in his *Notes from the Century Before*, a book about British Columbia, survivors of close encounters with the grizzly report that one of the bear's most objectionable features is its foul breath. Don't shoot until you can smell the *Ursus halitosis*. Autopsies reveal that many grizzlies suffer from stomach ulcers. Why? We don't know. Like us, the bear is omnivorous, will eat anything—even humans— that it can catch. Eats our baggage too. A lone hiker in Glacier National Park was destroyed and mostly consumed ("harvested") by a bear a few years ago. The victim was a recent convert to the Moral Majority and carried a Bible in his pack. The park rangers' investigation disclosed that the grizzly had eaten most of the Bible also.

The man had been forewarned, if he'd read his gospel. There is a passage in the Old Testament in which God sics a bear upon a pack of unruly children.

Some people do not approve of carrying firearms in grizzly country. Again I refer to Douglas Peacock, who has lived and worked on close terms with the great bear for twelve years: to carry a gun, he says, distorts the psychology of the situation, makes a man cocky, noisy, overconfident, careless, reducing the opportunity for frequent, close, and friendly relations with the grizzly. Doug says that he has been threatened many times and charged several times by nervous GRIZZ. He stands his ground, keeps talking in soft and mollifying tones, keeps on running his movie camera. So far the attacking bear has always turned aside before completing the charge, or soon enough to avoid losing face. "They decide I'm the dominant bear on the ridge," Doug says, standing over his campfire, smoking himself up in order to diminish the human scent. So far. Once a bear attacked his camp while Doug was away, ate his sleeping bag—a provocative act of inquiry. His study of the grizzly, he admits, is a two-way, mutual investigation. He hopes to finish his movie soon.

Doug Peacock usually works alone, responsible for nobody's

life but his own. Commercial outfitters like Mark Jensen, and professional wilderness guides like Dana Van Burgh, feeling responsible for the safety of their clients—who have come a long way at considerable financial expense to enjoy the mosquitoes, white-sock blackflies, GRIZZ, polar bears, Arctic wind chill, avalanches, wolves, swamps, drunken Eskimos on motorized tricycles, the ice and isolation and other varied pleasures of Alaska—always bring shotguns.

The noise we heard is not repeated. Dana and I surmise a lone caribou browsing on willow leaves. We finish our work. Erecting my own tent—an Oval Invention from North Face—out on the gravel bar close to the river, where the breeze is breezier and the mosquitoes scattered, I happen to glance up and see a file of caribou, ten, twelve, fifteen of them, moving rapidly down the open mountainside on the other side of the Kongakut valley. They appear to be heading for an acre field of overflow ice, the white *Aufeis*, as the Germans call it, which covers much of the bottomland a half mile to our north. I watch them for a while through my binoculars. Pale brown or yellowish in color, as big as elk, each animal carries an impressive rack of antlers (not horns) on its head, the cow and yearling as well as the bull. They look to me like storybook reindeer, exactly the kind that Santa Claus once harnessed to his sleigh. The caribou gather on the ice and linger there, perhaps to escape for a time the flying swarms of devils that infest the grass, flowers, shrubs, heather and bracken of the tundra-upholstered hillsides.

Heather, bracken—there is much about this open, spacious, treeless terrain that recalls Scotland, the Hebrides, the maritime provinces of eastern Canada. We are, after all, not far from the Beaufort Sea, the ice packs of the Arctic Ocean. White Thayer's gulls, winging back and forth across the river, reinforce the resemblance.

The Cessna returns, circles once, floats down upon the rough shingle of the gravel bar, bounces to another hair-raising stop in an aura of dust. Dana has hung his rainbow-colored paper carp on a pole, providing a wind sock, but when we made the first landing there was no such indicator available. "How," I had asked our pilot, young Gil Zemansky, Ph.D. (biology), "do you determine wind direction in a place like this?" Looking down as we circled the apparent landing spot—and *spot* is the right word—I could see nothing, not even a drift of dust, to suggest the proper approach.

"I go by the feel of the plane," Dr. Zemansky replied. This technique was formerly known as "flying by the seat of the pants." He added, "Sometimes you can see wind ripples on the water."

The airplane is opened from within, disgorging the pilot, our trip leader Mark Jensen, another half ton of baggage, and a lawyer. A lawyer on the Kongakut River? Everybody has to be somewhere, said the philosopher Parmenides, explaining his theory of the plenum. Her name is Ginger Fletcher, and she comes from Salt Lake City, where she works as a public defender. She's that kind of lawyer, public spirited, and a smart, lively, good-looking young woman to boot. (I list her more conspicuous attributes in random order of importance.) When she opens a bottle of schnapps from her bag, later that day, we name her Ginger Schnapps.

Like so many professional outdoors people, Mark Jensen is one of those depressing youngish types (thirty-four years old) with the body of a trained athlete, hands like Vise-Grips, a keen mind bright with ideas and full of enthusiasm for any project that promises the rewards of difficulty. He owns in fee simple the usual array of primary skills—being a first-class boatman, fisherman, hunter, camp cook, mountain climber, and so on and so forth. I'm sick of these *Übermenschen* and wish that Fran Leibowitz and Nora Ephron were here. My kind of folks. He has hair like Robert Redford, drinks Wild Turkey, and bears front and center on his face a sort of Robert Mitchum high-bridged nose, which gives him in profile the classical heroic Homeric look. Life is not fair. But in compensation he addresses everyone as "mate" or "partner," which fools no one.

Mark glances with approval at the standing cook tent, the twig fire crackling on its sheet-iron firepan, and says to his hired subordinate, "Coffee ready, mate?" Jensen is an insatiable coffee drinker.

Dana Van Burgh III is not overawed. "You forgot to pack it in the first load, blue eyes. You'll have to wait."

Jensen smiles, opens a big Thermos jug, and pours each of us a cupful of hot smoking coffee. Gil Zemansky gulps his quickly, we pivot his aircraft around by hand, nose into the wind, and off he roars in all-out effort, racketing over the stones and gravel at 60–80 MPH toward the willow thicket, the boulders, the river, departing earth as before at the last plausible moment. He has one more trip to make, three more passengers to bring us, before his work is done and the day ends. But of course, I remind myself, it's late June in the Arctic Zone; this day will not end, not for us. For us that sun never will go down.

We carry the baggage off the landing strip, build up the fire, start a two-gallon pot of coffee, eat a snack before supper. Or is it lunch? Ginger puts up her tent back in the caribou-cropped willows. We watch more caribou trickle over the mountain to join their friends on the ice field. A golden eagle sails overhead, and the gulls come and go, hoping for someone to catch and gut a fish. But seeing the growing assembly of caribou downriver, Mark Jensen and the others uncase their cameras and sneak that way, hoping for close-up photographs. I follow with binoculars.

I realize that I have described all of these people, including the pilot, as young. Compared to me they are. Everywhere I go these days I seem to find myself surrounded by younger and younger humans. If one keeps hanging about, as I do, then the temporal horizon expands, the pursuing generations extend toward infinity. But why should I care? Sagging into my late middle age, I have discovered one clear consolation for my stiffening back (I never could touch my toes anyway, and why should I want to?), my mildewed pancreas, my missing gall bladder, my *panza de cerveza*, my cranky and arthritic Anglo-Saxon attitudes. And the consolation is this—that I am content with my limitations.

The achievement of middle age is itself an achievement.

Unsuspecting, the caribou come to meet us, a herd of twenty-five or so. Anxious and bug-harassed creatures, they usually keep on the move. I can hear the lens shutters snapping in the thicket as the beasts splash through shallow water, approaching to within fifty feet of where I sit on the gravel beach. They pass me, their big ungulate feet clicking, then spot Dana's paper fish fluttering on its staff. They stop, turn, go the other way, finely attuned to one another's movements, ideas and opinions as a school of minnows. (Like literary critics.) Watching them at close range, I can see the velvet on their antlers, the large glowing eyeballs, the supple muscles, the spring and tension in their step. Each animal moves within its personalized cloud of gnats, flies, mosquitoes— every insect probing for entrance into an eye, nostril, ear, mouth, vagina, rectum or wound. I do not envy the caribou. North of here on the calving grounds, as we shall learn, the bear and wolves are attacking the newborn caribou at this very hour. The natives hound them on snowmobiles (or "snow machines," as Alaskans say), shooting them down by the thousands with high-powered, scope-sighted rifles ("subsistence hunting"). Even the golden eagle, according to some Alaska State Fish and Game officials, will attack and kill a caribou calf. Nobody envies the caribou. But like fruit flies, rabbits, alley cats, street rats and the human race, caribou possess one great talent for survival—not intelligence or the power of reasoning, but fertility, a high rate of reproduction.

The herd crosses the river again below the willow thicket, giving the photographers another chance at close pictures, and jogs in unison up the west side of the valley, beyond our camp. We return to campfire and coffee. Mark assembles his fly rod and goes fishing for char, not with a fly but a lure, the Luhr Jensen (made in Norway) "Krokodile," triple-hooked but without barbs. Mark has filed off the barbs. Anything he catches not big enough to be worth cooking and eating he can release and return to the river with minimal injury. Physical injury, I mean—who knows what psychic trauma the fish suffers? Experience suggests that refished fish are meaner, tougher, wilier than what one might call virginal fish.

Myself, I gave up fishing decades ago. Not so much on moral grounds—although I can see the point of animal liberationists when they argue that there is something unjust in fishing or hunting primarily for *sport*—but on account of sloth. I lack the diligence and industry to stand in one place for hours, casting and recasting, reeling in and reeling out, endeavoring to outwit a simple creature with a one-digit I.Q. and one-twentieth my body weight. In the time one man spends trying to catch one fish I have ascended a small mountain, explored five miles of river valley, or probed to its secret heart a winding desert canyon.

I don't even much like to eat fish. In the outback I am content with a diet of cereal and powdered milk for breakfast, a hunk of cheese or a stick of jerky for lunch, a can of pork and beans for supper.

But these are private prejudices. I am aware of the argument that hunting and fishing can lead a man into an intense, intimate engagement with the natural world unknown to the casual hiker. When the hunting or fishing is based on hunger, on need, I know that this is true. But sport, in the end, is only sport—*divertisse-ment*. A diversion, that is, from the central game of life. Which is—what? Let's not go into that. Furthermore, I have yet to taste the flesh of the fresh-baked Arctic char.

Once more our aerial taxicab returns, unloading the balance of the 1983 Kongakut expedition: John Feeley, a schoolteacher from a little town called Whittier in southern Alaska; a legal secretary named Maureen Bachman from Anchorage; and Mike Bladyka, an anesthesiologist from Los Angeles. Good people, happy to be here. Each of us but John has been on a river trip with Mark Jensen before. Obeying the territorial, nesting instinct, each sets up his tent first thing. Maureen moves in with Ginger. John uncases his rod and goes fishing, Mike joins the crowd in the cook tent, out of the wind, to manufacture the salad for our first wilderness dinner. I too do my part: I sit on my ammo can and activate my word processor. It's a good one. User-friendly, cheap, silent, no vibrations or radiation, no moving parts, no maintenance, no power source needed, easily replaceable, fully portable—it consists of a notebook and a ball-point pen from "Desert Trees, 9559 N. Camino del Plata, Tucson, Ariz." The necessary software must be supplied by the operator, but as friendly critics have pointed out, an author's head is full of that.

Mark fails to land a worthwhile fish. John also fails—in fact he loses half his tackle to a rock or submerged log or sunken fuel drum. They'll both do better in the days to follow. For dinner we get by on soup, salad, spaghetti and sauce with meatballs. We drink no beer on this trip. When air freight costs one dollar a pound, beer is not cost effective; we subsist on wine, whisky, schnapps, and best of all, the forty-degree-cold immaculately conceived waters of the Kongakut River.

Jensen passes on the meatballs. A semivegetarian, he refuses on nutritional grounds to eat beef and pork, asserting that in the ten years since giving up on what he calls "dead red" he has become a healthier, happier, more wholesome human being. He could be right about that, but the rest of us disregard his advice and eat the meatballs. Every time we eat a cow, I remind him, we save the life of a moose, two caribou, four mule deer, or eight char squared. He ponders the dilemma. I twist the knife: "Whose side are you on, Jensen? God's side, Saint Francis's side, John Muir's side, or the side of those rangeland lawn mowers we call beef cattle?"

"Beef is bad for you, partner," he insists. "Look at this stunted little runt Dana here, twenty-five years old and still not six foot high. Never will grow to man size."

Dana helps himself to a second helping of the entrée. "At least I'm not anemic. I can tie my shoes without gasping for air."

The sun angles sidewise behind some western peaks. But there is no sunset, no evening. Not even a twilight. The bald unmediated light continues to shine on the mountainsides east of the river. There are a couple of wristwatches in our group but no one refers to them. There seems no point to it. We plan to camp here for a second "day," a second "night." With only eighty miles of river to run and ten days to do it in, this should be a leisurely journey. We sit on the surplus ammunition cans, the sturdy Gott coolers, and talk and drink too much coffee and contemplate the golden midnight light in the land of the midnight sun. At last and reluctantly, one by one, we let the wind or the mosquitoes or fatigue—it's been a long day—worry us into our tents.

The light inside my translucent nylon dome is bright enough to read a book by. The mosquitoes gather outside the netting of my doorway, poking their Pinocchio noses through the interstices, sniffing at me like bloodhounds. A few have followed me inside. I hunt them down, one at a time, and pinch their little heads off. For such resolute, persistent, vicious, bloodthirsty animalcules, they are surprisingly fragile. As individuals. One slap on the snout and they crumple. Collectively they can drive a bull moose insane. I feel no remorse in extinguishing their miserable lives. I'm a coldhearted bleeding heart. Yet I know that even the mosquito has a function—you might say a purpose—in the great web of life. Their larvae help feed fingerlings, for example. Certain of their women help spread the parasitic protozoa that give us dengue, breakbone fever, yellow fever and malaria, for example, keeping in control the human population of places like Borneo, Angola, Italy and Mississippi. No organism can be condemned as totally useless.

Nevertheless, one does not wish them well. I would not kill them all, but I will certainly kill every one I can catch. Send them back where they came from.

We sleep. I dream that I hear robins, two hundred miles north of the Arctic Circle. Dreaming of Home, Pennsylvania.

∠

June 25—Today we climb a mountain. We follow a brook up a deep ravine, over the rocks and a deep-pile carpet of tundra, lupine, buttercups, forget-me-nots, campion, mountain avens, bayrose, eight-petal dryas, kinnikinnick, saxifrage ("stonebreakers"), woolly lousewort (a favorite of mine), Labrador tea, drunken bumblebees, piles of caribou droppings like chocolate-covered almonds, pictographic lichen on the limestone, and many little yellow composites. What are these? asks Ginger. Don't know, says Mark. Water gurgles under the rocks. Call it a virus, says Dana; that's what doctors do when they don't know. Ain't that right, Doc? Doctor Mike smiles, chuffing along with me in the rear guard of the party. Aside from myself, he is the only person here over the age of thirty-five.

We scramble up a pile of scree and eat lunch on the summit, twenty-five hundred feet above the river, five thousand feet above sea level. Snowy peaks lift hoary heads (as John Muir would say) in most—not all—directions. We are in that part of the Brooks Range called the Romanzof Mountains, which recalls the former colonizers of the Alaskan territory. To the Russians Alaska must have seemed like merely a two-bit extension of Siberia. Extreme East Slobbovia. No wonder they parted with it so cheaply.

Americans think Alaska is big. The Mackenzie Territory of northwest Canada is bigger. Siberia is several times bigger than both combined. So much for surface extension. If the state of Utah, which consists mostly of mountains, plateaus, mesas, buttes, pinnacles, synclines, anticlines, folds, reefs, canyons and vertical canyon walls were ironed out flat it would take up more room on a map than Texas. What does that prove? It's what is there, or here, now, that matters. So much for chauvinism. Most of the mountains around us, so far as we know, have never been climbed by anybody but the Dall sheep. The majority have not even been named, except for the most prominent, like Michelson (9,239 feet) and Chamberlin (9,131).

We return to camp by a different route, finding fresh bear sign on the way—torn-up sod, where the bear was rooting for marmots and ground squirrels; a well-trod bear trail; a messy pile of bear dung. Dana carries his shotgun slung on shoulder, but we stay alert as we march along. There is an animal out here that is bigger than we are. And *he* sings, as he rollicks along, "Yea, though I walk through the valley of the shadow of death I will fear no evil, for I am the evilest motherfucker in the valley."

We tramp through a mile of muskeg at the foot of the hills. Now we see what the rubber boots are for. Muskeg consists of tussocks of balled-up grass, each tussock the size of a human head, all rooted in a bog. The thoughtless locals down in Fairbanks call these unstable obstacles "nigger heads" but "Swede heads" would be more appropriate, for they are blond, straight haired, and long-headed. It is difficult to walk in the soft muck between them, even more difficult to walk upon or over them. Some "desert" this is. True, the average annual rainfall and snowfall is only between eight and ten inches. But the permafrost, the nearly universal permafrost, that hidden layer of never-thawing impermeable ice, prevents water from sinking below the surface of the ground. The North Slope is our swampiest desert; Alaska, our biggest, boggiest, buggiest state. We lurch and stumble through the mire, and as we advance great shimmering hosts of mosquitoes rise eagerly from the weeds to greet us. Dripping in sweat and the greasy oil of insect repellent, we stagger on. Takes guts to live in Alaska, no doubt about it. I am favorably impressed, once again, by the pluck and hardihood of these people, both native and white. I wonder though, sometimes, about their native intelligence.

We reach camp, the fresh breeze, the welcome hard ground of the gravel beach, wade into the icy river for a drink, then a shampoo, a bath—ladies upstream, men downstream.

Shivering in the wind, I dry myself with my cleanest dirty shirt. Forgot to bring a towel. The wind is coming up the river, as usual, from the north and the frozen Arctic Sea; I can feel that chill malignancy penetrate the marrow of my bones. Hurriedly I dress, layering on a shirt, a hooded sweatshirt and a parka. When I feel warm the wind stops.

And *they* come out again. I wait. One slap on the arm kills nine. Forgot to bring cigars. I reach for the repellent.

We have a Mexican dinner for supper, preceded by a pitcher of margaritas. The margaritas we ice with snow carried down from the mountain in a daypack by Mike, a thoughtful and foresighted man. We drink to his health. Life is rough on the Last Frontier. Don't feel quite right myself, but it's only a matter of acclimatizing: when I left Tucson three days ago the temperature was 106 in the shade; at Salt Lake City, where we paused for a day and a night, it was 65 degrees and stormy; at Fairbanks (elevation 440 feet), where I stayed for two nights, the air was hot, humid, muggy, close to 90 degrees, and hotter than that in my little cell at the El Sleazo Hotel on the banks of the Chena River; from Fairbanks by DC-3 to Barter Island, on the edge of the Arctic ice pack, we found ourselves in the heart of the wind-chill factory— even the Eskimos were wearing their parkas; and now on the river, where the wind comes and goes, the temperature seems to fluctuate from subfreezing to 80 and back again. But no one complains about the weather except me, and I do it inwardly only; can't let the others know that the most sissified rugged outdoorsman in the West is now squatting among them on his ammo can, huddled in thermal long johns, wool pants, wool shirt, flannel sweatshirt, wool ski cap, and a flannel-lined hooded parka.

Before turning in for the sun-bright night I requisition a handful of aspirins from the expedition infirmary; Mark also doses me with ten thousand milligrams of vitamin C and other huge jellied capsules, spansules and suppositories, each about horse-size. "Can't get sick on us, mate," he says; "you know there's no germs north of the Arctic Circle."

"Of course not," I agree. "But one could always show up." Crawling into my geodesic tent, sliding into my antique, greasy, duct-tape–mended mummy bag, I say to myself, No germs, eh? Well, if I was a germ I wouldn't want to live here either.

The sun shines all night long.

June 26—I awake by degrees to the sound of robins chirping in the cherry trees. Impossible. But when I emerge from my cocoon the first thing I see is a fat robin redbreast bouncing along on the gravel bar. How could such a small, harmless, innocent bird travel so far? Or, as Jensen says, how many FPM (wing flaps per minute) to cover three thousand miles?

Mark has caught an 18-inch char for breakfast; 4–5 pounds. He packs it with herbs and butter, wraps it in aluminum foil, and bakes it on a grill over the low driftwood fire. The flesh is firm, sweet, pink, something like fresh salmon but better, not so oily, much like the Dolly Varden we used to eat, years ago, from that little lake—Akakola—below the Numa Ridge fire lookout in Glacier Park. The Dolly Varden, in fact, is a type of char.

Today we plan to set out on the Kongakut. We inflate, rig and load the two neoprene rafts, strike tents, police the site. Like all good professional outfitters, Mark Jensen practices no-trace camping. Everything noncombustible is hammered flat with a stone and packed out. The ashes from the fire, collected on the metal firepan, are dumped into the river, where they will end their chemic lives blended with the Arctic Ocean. Even our footprints—since we've made camp on the floodplain—will be obliterated by the next rise in the river.

None of these measures is yet required by official regulations, although we are in the heart of the Arctic National Wildlife Refuge, a federal preserve. Mark does it because he believes in it, because it's right, and because we may be followed, someday, by others. And he takes the opportunity to grumble a bit about the Eskimos, Indians, trophy hunters, and oil-company exploration crews, who have left so much of Alaska littered with empty fuel drums, toilet paper, Pampers, whisky bottles, broken-down Ski-doos, Pop-Tart wrappers, tangled fishing tackle, Cat-train tracks, the swash plates and lag hinges from dilapidated helicopters.

Pampers? Oh yes, the plastic diaper is quite popular now with the natives. Universally used. Whereas the Alaskan women formerly employed fingers and tongues to clean their babies, they now prefer the synthetic substitute, like most mothers everywhere else (though cotton is better for babies' bottoms). Old ways die easily—they tumble over themselves in a *rush* to die—when confronted by the frills of high-tech Western civilization. However, it does seem hypocritical of the natives to complain, as they eagerly embrace the worst of our culture, that we are destroying the best of theirs. They can't have it both ways. The role of victim can be pushed too far. There even may be a limit to the white-liberal-guilt neurosis.

Back off, mate. You're stepping on taboos again. I can hear the stir and crackling of tired old middle-class hackles rising all around me.

We launch forth onto troubled waters. Check the time by Maureen's quartz crystal wristwatch: 2:00 P.M., Fairbanks time. We have again failed to crack the noon barrier. But here where high noon lasts for hours, it does not matter.

We float downstream through the treeless hills, among the golden tundra mountains. It's something like boating through

Colorado at thirteen thousand feet. We see golden plovers out on the flats, another golden eagle overhead. And the gulls. And the robins. And a raven.

"My favorite bird," says Mark. "Smart, talented, handsome—"

"Like you," says Ginger.

"Like me. When I—" He points to the high mountainside on our left. "Sheep."

A herd of Dall sheep are grazing up there, a dozen of them—ewes, lambs, rams with curling horns. Placid, motionless, they watch us—phantom beings out of nowhere—drifting through their world.

"When I come back," continues Mark, "I want to come back as a raven."

"Crawling with lice," Ginger points out. "Smelling like a dead fish."

"With a beak even bigger than the beak you've got now," says Maureen. "Proportionately speaking."

Smiling, Mark stands up between the oars to survey the channel ahead. Like most Alaskan rivers, the Kongakut is a shallow river, broad and braided, hard to read, forcing the boatman to search constantly for the one navigable channel among many false options. We'll portage twice before this voyage is done, and jockey the boats several times over submerged gravel bars. Following us in the second boat, Dana watches carefully. Only Mark has seen this river before.

All goes well today. In the evening we make camp on another bar, a pleasant site with limestone cliffs overlooking the river, a grove of little ten-foot cottonwoods on the other shore, a vista upriver of the valley we have come through and the splendid craggy snowy mountains beyond. The classic Alpine-Arctic scene —photogenic, fundamental, perfect.

Why are there almost no trees on the north slope of the Brooks? Because of the permafrost two feet below the surface, a substratum of rocklike ice, which prevents trees from sinking roots. Only close to the river, where the ground is warmer, can the dwarf willows and midget cottonwoods take hold.

Years ago I was employed briefly as a technical writer for the Western Electric Company in New York City. The company had a contract with the War Department to prepare training manuals for the workers building the Arctic radar stations and air bases of the Distant Early Warning system. One hundred of us sat at desks in one huge office ten floors above Hudson Street in lower Manhattan. Fluorescent lights glared down upon our bent, white-shirted backs. (All technical writers were required to wear white shirts. With tie.) Since my security clearance had not yet come through, I was assigned the menial task of editing the manual called *How to Dispose of Human Sewage in Permafrost*. I told the boss I wanted to be sent to the Arctic in order to conduct first-hand field studies. He told me that my job was spelling, grammar and punctuation, not shit research. I returned to my desk among the other stuffed bent white shirts—we all faced in the same direction—and stared moodily out the window for two weeks, watching the sun go down over Hoboken, New Jersey.

The boss came to me. "Abbey," he says, "do you really want to work for Western Electric?" "No sir," I said, "not really." "I thought not," he said; "we're letting you go as of seventeen hundred hours today." I could have kissed him—and knowing New York, I probably should have. "That's all right, sir," I said, "I'm leaving right now, as of thirteen-thirty hours." And I did. Spent the afternoon at the White Horse Tavern on Hudson Street, then with cronies at Minsky's Burlesque in Newark. Reported to my wife, drunk and happy, at twenty-two hundred hours with what was left of my first and final Western Electric paycheck. Pointed the old Chevy pickup south and west at twenty-three hundred hours headed for Arizona. Never did learn how to dispose of human sewage (is there any other kind?) in permafrost.

But I know now. As I discovered on Barter Island, they dump

it into a sewage lagoon two feet deep, chlorinate the water and drink it. And how do they dispose of general garbage on the North Slope? They don't; they leave it on the surface, where it becomes the highest and most scenic feature of the landscape.

Beef stroganoff for supper. The Russian influence lingers on in nostalgia-loving Alaska.

Loaded with aspirin and more of Jensen's horse medicine, I retire early to my tent, still not feeling too good. Forgot to bring a towel, forgot the cigars, forgot to bring a book. So I borrow a paperback from Maureen—something called *Still Life with Woodpecker*? Yes, that appears to be the title. I glance at the blurbs, the summary on the back cover. "You didn't bring anything for grown-ups?" She has not. "Did anybody?" I ask the group.

Dana offers me a book called *The Dancing Wu Li Masters* by a Mr. Gary Zukav. Another California-type book. "How about a Gideon's Bible? Or a dictionary?" Mark offers his ammo-can edition of Merriam-Webster's. "Already read that one," I say. I borrow the first two, churlish ungrateful bastard, and skulk off. The wind has died; a number of dancing Wu Li masters follow me into my tent. I slaughter them and bed down with Tom Robbins and Mr. Gary Zukav. *Mènage a trois . . . de poupée . . . entente . . .*

I was sick for the next two days.

🕊

June 27—Morning, so to speak. Mark asks me how I'm feeling. "Great!" I say, lying through the skin of my eyeteeth.

"You sure?"

"For Chrissake, Jensen, I was sleeping in elk pastures when you were wearing Pampers in the sixth grade."

"We can stay here another day, you know. Lots of time."

"To hell with that. Down the river! Onward!"

Breakfast goes by in a blur. We load the boats, shove off, glide down the current between walls of turquoise-colored *Aufeis*. An ice gulch. Horned white sheep, like woolly maggots, crawl upon the distant hillsides. Clouds cover the sun; the Arctic wind comes sweeping up the river. Dana strains at the oars, sweating hard to keep up with Mark while I sit huddled in the bow swaddled in layers of Pendleton and polyester and self-pity. Dana tries to keep the conversational hacky-sack in the air, working manfully to maintain both civility and headway against the wind. "Let me know if you see a GRIZ," I growl, nodding off. He nods.

Hours pass, along with some gravel bars, a few willow thickets, more walls of ice. This is the kind of thing, I say to myself, that no one actually wants to do. And afterward you're not even glad you did it. Unlike the infantry, or suicide, or exploratory surgery. I become aware of danger ahead. Trouble: I look up hopefully.

Mark has beached his rubber raft on a most unlikely, rough, and difficult spot. Emphatically he signals Dana to bring his boat alongside. "Ready for a fast landing," Dana says, pulling hard toward shore. I pick the coiled bowline from under my rubber boots. We grate onto the ice and gravel, I stagger out with the rope and hold the boat against the violent tug of the current. Dana jumps out, we heave the boat higher onto the gravel. There is nothing here to tie up to: all hands are summoned to drag both boats out of the river.

Mark talks quietly with Dana. Followed by John, they go off to investigate something ahead. All that I can see, from where we have landed, is the river funneling into a narrow channel between vertical walls of blue ice six to ten feet high. Fifty yards ahead the river swerves around a bend, going out of view within the icy walls. We have stopped at the last possible takeout point short of a full commitment to the ice canyon.

"What seems to be the trouble here?" I say, holding out my GI canteen cup. Ginger is pouring hot coffee from the Thermos jug. My hands shake with cold; I need both hands to hold my cup steady.

"Don't know," she says. "Mark said he doesn't like the looks of the river here."

"Looks like the same old Styx to me," Mike says from deep within his parka hood. I'm glad to see that he too is feeling the cold. Los Angeles. He and I, the only southwesterners in the party, are equally thin blooded.

Mark, Dana, John come back. Mark looks somber, an unusual expression for his habitually cheerful face. "We'll camp here, mates."

"Here? On the ice?"

He points to the left bank, beyond the ice. "Over there." We unload the boats and carry our gear and baggage to dry land, then come back for the boats. By then we've seen what the problem is. Not far beyond the bend the river goes *under* the ice, emerging a hundred feet beyond. If we had gone on in the boats we would have been trapped and drowned beneath the ice, or if flushed through, probably died of hypothermia before we found dry matches and sufficient wood to get a big fire going.

"I had this feeling," Mark says.

Most of the party get out cameras for pictures of the ice tunnel. I pitch my tent and creep inside. Aspirins and river water and sleep for me. I am awakened frequently through the long hours that follow by the roar of huge chunks of ice calving from the frozen walls, crashing into the river.

Warm weather again. By breakfast time, which by now has slipped to ten or eleven in the morning, the ice tunnel is reduced to a narrow ice bridge. Then the bridge collapses, sending a small tidal wave upstream over the gravel bar on which we've erected the cook tent and camp headquarters. But no damage is done and the river is again clear.

June 28—I totter down the hill from my tent and join the jolly bunch around the breakfast fire. Mutely, sadly, I hold out my tin cup; someone pours coffee into it. "How's it going, partner?" our leader says.

"Great," I mumble, "great."

"You don't look good," he says. "In fact you look sick. Time for more horse capsules, mate."

I swallow the jellied suppositories and watch Ginger and Mike squabbling politely over Mark's last blueberry pancake. You take it, she says. Naw, you take it, Mike says. They remind me, in my fluish delirium, of my friend Kevin Briggs, another river rat, and of his parable of the last pork chop.

My friend Kevin is a stout, husky fellow with a vigorous appetite. Being a graduate student of philosophy and literature he is always hungry. One day he and five classmates were invited to lunch by their teacher, Ms. Doctor Professor H _____. A kind, well-meaning but frugal woman, Professor H _____ seated her six guests at the dining table in her home and set a platter holding exactly seven pork chops at the head of the table. Kevin, seated on her right, too hungry to waste time counting the pork chops, helped himself to two from the top and passed the platter on. Professor H _____ meanwhile had gone back to her kitchen. She returned with the mashed potatoes and gravy just as the platter had nearly completed its round of the table. One pork chop remained. She sat down. The young man on her left, who had not yet served himself, looked at the last pork chop, then at his hostess. She looked at him. Both laughed, awkwardly. You take it, he said. Oh no, she said, you take it. I'm really not hungry, he said. I'm not either, really, she said. Kevin by this time had gobbled down everything on his plate; he reached across the table with his fork and stabbed the last pork chop. I'll eat it, he said. And he did.

Moral? He who hesitates is second? No, Kevin explained to me, not at all. Remember the words of our Lord and Savior: "To him that hath much, much shall be given. But verily, from him that hath little, that little shall be taken away." (*Matthew, X:xii.*)

Mark Jensen, looking at me, says, "We'll stay here a couple of days. Who wants to climb another mountain?"

I creep back to my tent. I read the borrowed books.

I cough, I blow my nose, I read and finish *Still Life with Wood-pecker* and try to imagine what the typical Tom Robbins reader (and there are millions) must be like. Well, first of all, she would be about twelve years old. She? No, it. *It* is about twelve years old, a thoroughly homogenized androgyne of neuter sex. It lives in California or north-central New Mexico, also likes Rod Mc-Kuen, studies kundalini yoga, loves stuffed koala bears, thinks the *Whole Earth Catalog* is a book, believes Bob "Dylan" is a poet and Neil Diamond a musician, disdains politics as "too political" and . . . enough! The soul staggers, sinking deep into the swampy muskeg of pop Kultur. Put it this way: one spoonful of Tom Robbins's prose is enough to sicken the mind for hours. To read a Tom Robbins book from end to end is like chugalugging a quart of Aunt Jemima's pancake syrup. Or like—like the time a Supai Indian and I were stranded for two days at the head of Topocoba Trail at Grand Canyon waiting for a truck that arrived two days late. We had nothing with us to eat, absolutely nothing, but a straw basket full of overripe figs. We ate them.

We should have eaten the basket, fed the figs to the horses.

I crawl from my tent on hands and knees, vomit on a harmless cluster of forget-me-nots, state flower of Alaska (there are flowers everywhere on the tundra in the bright, jocund Arctic spring), crawl back in the tent and open *The Dancing Wu Li Masters.* The title is not encouraging but I am sure that I will find something nice to say about this book. I have never met a book yet that did not have *something* good about it.

Until now.

Hours later I am stirred from a deep stupor by Mark Jensen, bringing me with his own hands a bowl of hot celery soup and a plate containing chunks of fish with noodles and mashed potatoes. It looks good and I am hungry.

"How's it going, partner?"

"Fine, Mark, fine. Say, this is damn good fish. You catch another char?"

"That's turkey. Out of a can."

"Damn good. See any GRIZZ?"

"Had a glimpse of one going over the next ridge. Only for a minute. A true silvertip—we could see the fur shining on the shoulder hump. You should've been there, mate."

"I know. What else?"

"Lots of sheep. A wolf. A lone bull caribou."

"Sure sorry I missed that bear."

"We thought of you, mate. If I'd had a good rope with me I'd have lassoed the son of a bitch and led him back here. Better take some more of these pharmaceuticals."

![symbol]

June 30—Another gay, sunny, brisk, breezy Arctic morning. We carry the boats to the river, since the river will not come to us, and proceed as before, downstream. My flu has entered its terminal phase, and I am ready to meet my Maker, eyeball to eyeball, way up here on top of the world, as we say in these parts.

The top of the world. But of course, the giddy, dizzying truth is that the words "top" and "bottom," from a planetary point of view, have no meaning. From out here in deep space, where I am orbiting, there is no top, there is no bottom, no floor, no ceiling, to anything. We spin through an infinite void, following our curving path around the sun, which is as bewildered as we are. True, the infinite is incomprehensible—but the finite is absurd. Einstein claimed otherwise, I know, but Einstein was only a mortal like us. No ceiling, no floor, no walls. . . . We are 250 miles north of the Arctic Circle, and we flow as we go, like spindrift, like bits of Styrofoam, through the outliers of what Mark says is the northernmost mountain range in the world, i.e., on Earth. Will we ever get back to downtown Kaktovik?

I think of the Eskimos, holed up all day inside their $250,000 air-freighted prefab modular houses (paid for with oil royalties), watching "Mr. Rogers' Neighborhood" on their brand-new color TV sets. A few grinning kids race up and down the dirt street, among the melting snowbanks, on their Honda ATCs. What we call "road lice" back in the Southwest. (Girls love horses. Little boys love machines. Grown-up men and women like to walk.) The kids seem to have nothing else to do. A dead bowhead whale—rare species—lies rotting on the waterfront, partially dismembered. Slabs of whale blubber—muktuk—are stacked in the yard of each house, along with empty plywood crates, diesel spills, oil drums, Ski-doo parts, caribou antlers, musk-ox bones, wolf pelts, moose heads, worn-out rubber boots, tin cans and liquor bottles and loose papers and plastic potsherds. In each yard lies one howling arthritic Huskie dog, token souvenir of former days, short-chained to a stake, out of reach of the muktuk. The dogs are never released from the chain.

When I entered the village store to buy some good cheap mosquito-repellent cigars I found the shelves loaded with cartons and cases of Pepsi-Cola, candy bars, Holsum bread, sweet rolls, cigarettes, Oreo cookies, Cheezits, Coleman fuel, propane bottles, not much else. No cigars. The manager of the store is a white man. The village post office (ZIP code 99747) is operated by a young white woman. The teachers in the ten-million-dollar school are all whites. When something goes wrong with the village plumbing or electricity (the steady bellow of diesel generators, louder than wind, makes a constant background noise at Kaktovik and Barter Island), as happens frequently, private contractors—white men—are flown in from Fairbanks or Anchorage, at enormous expense, to repair the damage. This has nothing to do with race discrimination; the natives don't want the jobs.

And the wind blows day and night, forever, out of the north, from beyond the dead whale on the beach, from beyond the mangled ice floes, out of the infinite wastes of the most awesome sight in the North: that pale cold no-man's-land, that endless frozen desert of ice leading as far as eye can perceive out over the Beaufort Sea and into the Arctic Ocean. Toward the Pole.

What will happen to these people when the North Slope oil gives out? The Eskimos and other Alaskan natives still enjoy the hunt, as much or more than ever, and when they do go hunting, on their screaming packs of snow machines, they kill everything that moves. (The musk-ox, for example, had to be reintroduced from Canada into the Arctic Wildlife Refuge because the natives, equipped with white man's machines and armed with white man's weapons, had exterminated the local herds.) But this kind of hunting, whether of land animals or of seals, whales, fish, polar bear, is entirely dependent upon technology. Impossible to imagine, I was told, that the new generations would or could return to the traditional nomadic way, following the game in its seasonal migrations from Alaska to Canada and back, surviving in hide tents and sod huts under the snow as their ancestors—their still-living grandparents—had done. Unimaginable. They'll all move to the slums of Fairbanks, Anchorage and Seattle, join the public-welfare culture, before consenting to such romantic humiliation. Can't blame them; until the coming of the white man the natives spent half their lives on the edge of starvation. Famine was common. Now, despite alcoholism, violence, suicide, their population is growing—and fast.

But we are told—and sometimes by the natives themselves—that they were a stronger, happier people before. They certainly don't appear to be happy now.

What happens to these people when they migrate to the city? I think of "Two Street" (Second Avenue), Fairbanks, which resembles the center of Flagstaff or Gallup on a Saturday night. There is even a "Navajo Taco Stand" on one corner, selling genuine Athapaskan tacos (fry bread, shredded lettuce, and hamburger), and the street is lined with grim little bars jam-packed with brawling Indians and Eskimos. Drunken aborigines lean on the walls outside, sit on the sidewalks, stumble toward the taxicab lineup to get a four-block ride home to some chain-saw shanty on the edge of town. Half conscious, they stare at you through eyes the complexion of strawberries, and try to bum a dollar. I saw one man *descamisado*, naked from the waist up, staggering down the street with one foot on the sidewalk and the other in the gutter; he looked confused.

Trying to look friendly I stepped into the doorway of a bar, thinking I needed a beer. One glance inside and I knew this was no place for an innocent white boy from the far south. The bar was lined wall-to-wall with dark, sullen, hostile faces, and in the middle of the floor two five-foot three-hundred-pound Athapaskan women stood toe-to-toe socking the piss out of each other. Just like down home: the Club 66 in Flag, the Eagle in Gallup, or the Silver Dollar in Bluff, on the edge of the Navajo reservation—the only bar in Utah where you can hear squaw dance music on the jukebox. I withdrew. The sights, the smells and the noise were making me homesick.

The bars in Alaska are legally open twenty-one hours a day. From 5:00 A.M. to 8:00 A.M. they are required by law to close. It is then, say the white locals, that you'll see "the moles crawl out of their holes."

Resentment on one side, contempt on the other: the race war in Alaska looks as promising as it does most everywhere else on our overpopulated, much-abused, ever-percolating planet.

Les misanthropes must love it here.

Back, for godsake, *back*—to the decency and the sanity of the wild river. If there is a civilized society left anywhere on Earth it exists among the caribou, the wolves, the eagles, the bighorn and the moose of the Kongakut.

We camp today at a broad open place that Mark has named Velvet Valley. Under a spiny, purple, crenellated mountain that looks like Mordor, like the Hall of the Mountain King, like Darth Vader's childhood playpen, like the home of the Wicked Witch of the North, extends a lovely valley clothed in golden tundra, a million bloody blooming flowers, the lambent glowing light of the midnight sun. (I dislike that word *lambent*, but it must be employed.) A soft, benevolent radiance, you might say, playing upon the emerald green, the virgin swales of grass and moss and heather and Swede heads.

The Arctic wind blows merrily; it takes four of us to get the cook tent up, our only communal shelter. Feeling a mite better now, I scrounge for firewood with the others, and soon we've got a good fire burning near the entrance to the tent, a big meal under way inside.

More time slippage. We'd eaten lunch at five in the afternoon, we're having dinner at eleven. Time, says Einstein, is a function of space. Or time, said another philosopher, is but the mind of space. How true. And is everything finally only relative? It is not. The light is fixed and absolute. Especially the Arctic light. We'll eat dinner at eleven and have a midnight snack in Seward's Icebox at four in the morning if we bloody well feel like it. Who's to stop us?

The sun shines all night long.

✎

July 2—John and Mark catch a big char and a small grayling for breakfast. A fine kettle of fish.

We go for a walk up the Velvet Valley, through the willows, through the muskeg, up onto the tundra, deep into the valley. Flowers everywhere, each flower concealing a knot of mosquitoes, but we're accustomed to the little shitheads by now; they don't bother us. We rub on the bug juice and let the insects dance and hover—patterns of organic energy made visible—in futile molecular orbits one inch from the skin. Like the flies in Australia the mosquitoes here become simply part of the atmosphere, the décor, the ambience. We ignore them.

A ram watches us from a high point of rock; his flock grazes above. Mark kneels by a mountain stream trying to photograph the crosshatched ripples of converging currents. Dana glasses the high ridges for bear, shotgun at his side. John is fishing back at the river. Mike, Maureen and Ginger are eating cheese and crackers and identifying the many flowers (with the help of a guidebook) that I have not mentioned. I sit on the grass scribbling these notes, with a clump of Siberian asters fluttering at my elbow.

This is what I am writing:

Alaska is not, as the state license plate asserts, "the Last Frontier." Alaska is the final big bite on the American table, where there is never quite enough to go around. "We're here for the megabucks," said a construction worker in the Bunkhouse at Kaktovik, "and nothing else." At the Bunkhouse the room and board costs $150 per day, on the monthly rate, but a cook can earn $10,000 a month. Others much more. Alaska is where a man feels free to destroy an entire valley by placer mining, as I could see from the air over Fairbanks, in order to extract one peanut-butter jar full of gold dust. Flying from Barter Island to the Kongakut, pilot Gil Zemansky showed me the vast spread of unspoiled coastal plain where Arco, Chevron, and others plan oil and gas exploration in the near future, using D-7 bulldozers pulling sledges, thus invading the caribou calving grounds and tearing up the tundra and foothills of the Arctic Wildlife Refuge, last great genuine wilderness area left in the fifty United States. Under the heavy thumb of James Watt, the Fish and Wildlife Service apparently has no choice but to knuckle under to the demands of the oil industry. In southeast Alaska the industrial tree farmers who now run the U.S. Forest Service are allowing the logging companies to clearcut and decimate vast areas of the Tongass National Forest, home of our national bird, the bald eagle, and officially, ostensibly, the legal property of the American public—all of us. With Dracula placed in charge of the blood bank (as Congressman Morris Udall has said), Alaska, like the rest of our public domain, has been strapped down and laid open to the lust and greed of the international corporations. "Last Frontier"? Not exactly: Anchorage, Fairbanks, and outposts like Barter Island, with their glass-and-aluminum office buildings, their airlift prefab fiberboard hovels for the natives and the workers, their compounds of elaborate and destructive machinery, exhibit merely the latest development in the planetary expansion of space-age sleaze—not a frontier but a high-technology slum. For Americans, Alaska is the last pork chop.

What then is a frontier? The frontier, in my view, is that forgotten country where men and women live with and by and for the land, in self-reliant communities of mutual aid, in a spirit of independence, magnanimity and trust. (As Henry Thoreau once said.) A few people, but not many—few of the natives and even less of the whites—still attempt to inhabit Alaska in such a manner. The majority, it appears, or at least the majority of the vocal and powerful, are here for the profits. For the megabucks.

↙

July 3—Down the river, through the portal of the mountains into the foothills, approaching the coastal plain, we float northward in our little air-filled boats. Seeing that I have come back to life, the literary natives on shipboard badger me with bookish questions. I am happy to oblige.

What's the best book about Alaska? The best book about the North, I say, is *The Call of the Wild*. In the words of a critic, Jack London captures there the essence of the mythos of the wilder-

ness. No, she says, I mean about Alaska? *Winter News*, I say, by
John Haines—pure poetry; and by "pure" I mean poetry about
ordinary things, about the great weather, about daily living experience, as opposed to technical poetry, which is concerned
mainly with prosody, with technique (one of my favorite lectures).
Don't lecture me, she says, I'm talking about prose—about books
in prose. (I sense a trap about to snap.) What's the best prose
book about Alaska? I pause for a moment, pretending to reflect,
and say *Going to Extremes* by Joe McGinniss. A brilliant book.
Mandatory for anyone who wants a sense of what contemporary
life in Alaska is like. My opinion does not set well with the locals.
No! they say, McGinniss writes only about the sensational. Alaska
is a sensational place, I reply. He's a scandalmonger, they say.
Alaska is a scandalous place, I say; McGinniss tells the truth.
How much time have you spent in Alaska? they want to know.
About four weeks, all told, I answer. They smile in scorn. Four
weeks of observation, I explain, is better than a lifetime of daydreaming. What about *Coming into the Country*? someone asks.
I had to admit that I had started on that book but never finished
it. More questions. I say, since I left Cherry Tree down in Tennes-
see, this is the first time I've been warm. McPhee, I explain, is a
first-rate reporter, but too mild, too nice, too cautious—no point
of view. You like Robert Service? I love him. But, says my first
inquisitor, I don't think you really love Alaska, do you? The most
attractive feature of Alaska, I say, is its small, insignificant human
population, thanks to the miserable climate. Thanks a lot, she
says. I like the mountains, the glaciers, the wildlife, and the
roominess, I hasten to add—or I would if the bugs would stop
crowding me. I think you are a geographical chauvinist, she says;
a spatial bigot. Special? Spatial. Well, I confess, I'll admit I've
lived too long in the Southwest; I should have saved that for last.
Then what are you doing in Alaska? she says.

Me?

You.

Slumming, I explain.

Quiet, whispers Mark, resting on the oars. Look over there.

We look where he points. Three wolves are watching us from another bar beside the river, less than a hundred feet away. Three great gray shaggy wolves, backlit by the low sun, staring at us. Silently we drift closer. Gently, Mark pulls the boat onto the gravel, where it stops. Don't get out, Mark whispers. The wolves watch, the cameras come out, the wolves start to move away into the willow thicket and toward the open tundra. A whistle stops the last one as it climbs the bank. I stare at the wolf through my binoculars, the wolf stares at me; for one, still, frozen, sacred moment I see the wild green fire in its eyes. Then it shrugs, moves, vanishes.

We drift on, silently, down the clear gray waters. After a while my friend says to me, When's the last time you saw something like that in Arizona? In your whole crowded, polluted Southwest?

Me?

You.

Moi?

Vous.

Another pause. Never did, I say.

You ought to be ashamed of yourself.

I am.

You ought to take back everything you've said.

I take it all back. (*But*, I think, all the same . . .)

Now the river tangles itself into a dozen different channels, all shallow. The main channel runs straight into a jungle of willow. We unload the boats, portage them and our gear around the obstruction. As I'm lugging two ten-gallon ammo cans across the damp silt I see a pair of tracks coming toward me. Big feet with claw marks longer than my fingers. The feet are not so long as mine but they are twice as wide. Double wides, size 10-EEEE. I stop and look around through the silence and the emptiness.

Old Ephraim, where are you?

He does not appear.

We go on. We camp for the day and the daytime night at what Mark calls Buena Vista—a grand view upriver of the Portal, Wicked Witch Mountain, the hanging glaciers of the high peaks beyond. Charbroiled char for supper. A female char, and Mark has saved the pinkish mass of hard roe for possible use as bait. "Ever eat fish eggs?" I ask him.

"I ate caviar once," he says.

"Only once?"

"Once was enough."

I'm inclined to agree; once was enough for me too. Caviar is cold, salty, slimy stuff—tastes like fish eggs. As Shakespeare says, caviar is for the general; let him eat it.

John and I go for a long walk into the hills, over the spongy tundra, taking one of the shotguns with us. Peacock can face his bear with only a camera; I want firepower. As we walk uphill toward the sun we see the mosquitoes waiting for us, about two and a half billion of them hovering in place above the field, the little wings and bodies glowing in the sunlight. "It looks like a zone defense," John says. But they part before us, lackadaisical atoms unable to make up their pinpoint minds, yielding before our scent and our more concentrated nodules of organic energy, as Alan Watts would say.

John is a quiet fellow, likable, attractive despite his Yasser Arafat–type beard. He tells me a little about life in Whittier, Alaska. To get to his classroom in winter he walks from his bachelor apartment in a dormitory through an underground tunnel to the adjacent but separate school building. The wind outside, he says, would knock you down; when there is no wind the snow comes up to your armpits. Yet Whittier is in the far south of central Alaska—the balmy part. (You have to be balmy to live there.) When the one road out of town is closed he buckles on touring skis and glides five miles over the pass to the railway station for a ride to the heart of Anchorage. He likes his life in Whittier. (He says.) Likes his students, the bright and lively Indian kids. Doesn't mind the isolation—he's a reader of books. Is fond of snow, ice, wind, mountains, the soft summer—bugs and icicles both. "How long do you plan to stay there?" I ask him.

"Oh, another year, maybe two."

"Then where?"

"Oh . . . back to the other world."

❧

July 4—Mark celebrates with four blasts of the shotgun, shattering the morning air. Thinking a GRIZ is raiding the camp, I go running back only to see Mark and the others drinking coffee around the fire. Mark is always drinking coffee, and he makes strong coffee, stout and vigorous, powerful enough to deconstipate a sand-impacted Egyptian. "Listen, mate," he says, explaining his secret formula, "you don't need near as much water to make coffee as some people think."

John stands by the river with his camera, photographing another dead fish. He lost most of his rod to the Kongakut days ago but didn't let that stop him; he attached his reel and a new line to his rod case and went on fishing. We've had char and grayling coming out our ears for a week. We're up to our asses in fish. But good—beats bacon and beans by a country mile. And I *like* bacon and beans.

Last stop on the river. We're encamped at the place known as Caribou Pass, near another straight gravel bar on which Gil Zemansky will land to pick us up for the last flight to Barter Island, where we then will catch, tomorrow we hope, the Air North DC-3 for the journey over the Brooks Range to Fairbanks and points south.

Caribou Pass—but where are the caribou? They're supposed to be massing out on the coast one hundred thousand strong. So far the biggest bunch we've seen was twenty-five head. But here is where they should pass, through these low hills, on their annual trip into the Yukon and south from there to the edge of the forest, where they spend—where they endure, somehow—the dark and six-month-long Yukon winter.

On the hill above us, a mile away, stands a white wall-tent and a little below it four small bivouac tents—Bear Camp. A squad of wildlife students from the University of Alaska is living up there, trapping (alive) and identifying the rodents in the tundra, watching for the caribou herds, the wolves, the GRIZZ. Mark has told them about my grizzly problem, and when a young, blond-haired, brown-skinned man named Mike Phillips comes rushing down the hillside I climb up the hill to meet him. "A male grizzly," he reports, "one mile east of Bear Camp." He rushes up the hill, I trudge after him. When I get there, on the high point, the bear has disappeared. "Down in that willow thicket along the creek," says Mike, pointing. We glass the area for an hour but the bear is gone. "Probably took off behind the ridge," Mike explains, "and ambled over the divide." Of course, I think, it would, knowing that I was coming.

"The grizzly bear," I explain to Mike, "is apocryphal, like the griffin, the centaur, and the yeti."

"You wouldn't think so," he replies, "if you'd been with me two days ago." And he tells me about the scene at the caribou birthing grounds, the leisurely arrogant grizzlies he'd observed circling the great herd, chasing the cows and devouring some of the newborn young.

We watch for another hour, but the grizzly does not show. I return to the river. There I find my own party staring at a spectacle two miles away on the hillside west of the river. A big herd of caribou, two thousand, three thousand of them, a compact animal mass, is advancing steadily to the south. If they go up the side valley over there they'll be blocked by the mountains; if they come our way they'll have to pass within a quarter mile of where we stand, waiting and hoping.

But something, we can't see what, spooks the herd, and after milling in confusion for a few minutes they reach consensus and reverse direction, returning north the way they had come, jogging along at a smart pace. Within ten minutes the entire herd is out of sight. The caribou, like the grizzly bear, is unpredictable. They refuse to be guided by precedent or reason or common sense or the wishes of a delegation of tourists.

"When you have a steering committee of three thousand chairpersons," says Dr. Mike sadly, "you never know what is going to happen." He limps about on stocking feet—injured his right foot two days ago. "It's like Proposition Thirteen."

"You see the racks on those bulls?" says John. "And those Dall rams—a trophy hunter would go crazy here."

Yes he would. Fly in, set down, bag the biggest bull, the finest ram, hack off the head, leave the meat to waste *in situ*, fly out, go home, mount head on rumpus-room wall. Is there anything lower, I ask myself, than a trophy hunter? Think hard. Put your mind to it. But all I can think of is squid shit.

An albino mosquito sets down on my forearm. She walks nervously back and forth on my naked skin, searching for the ideal pore to probe for blood. I wait. She selects a spot she likes, the needle nose, like the drooping snout of a supersonic jet, comes down and enters. Slight prickling sensation. I hear a definite gurgling sound—but no, I must be imagining that. I am about to slap the little thing into eternity, into its next cycle on the meat wheel of life, when something stays my hand. Let this little one live, a voice says in my inner ear. Just once, be merciful. I hesitate. Another voice says, Don't let that Buddhist karma run over your Darwinian dogma: mash the brute. But still I hesitate, and as I do, the tiny albino withdraws her dildo, waggles her wings, and floats off into the mob. God only knows what ghastly plague I may have loosed upon humanity and the caribou by letting that one go. But I feel sort of good about it.

We deflate and unrig the rafts, roll them up into snug bundles, stack boats, oars, rowing frames, ammo boxes, rubber bags, icebox, tents and other dunnage at the downwind end of the imaginary airstrip.

The Cessna comes, Gil Zemansky at the controls, and the ferry operation to Barter Island begins. Mark assigns me the third and final flight, giving me four extra hours on the shore of the Kongakut. Last chance. Last chance for what? I know what but dare not bait the gods by even thinking of it. Last chance for an understanding with the spirit of the Arctic, that's what.

We wait. The plane comes and goes again with most of the cargo and all passengers but Maureen, John and I. Two more hours.

John sleeps. Maureen is reading a book and watching the hills and meditating. I go for a walk beside the river, over the gravel bars and through the willow, heading north. The cold green waters rush past at my side, breaking over the rocks with a surflike turbulence, bound for the northern sea. A mile beyond the airstrip I am cut off by a headland. I stop and look back. The shining river races toward me. The velvet-covered hills rise on either side, the great jagged wall of the Brooks extends across the southern horizon—seven hundred miles of largely unknown mountains, reaching across Alaska from the Yukon to the Bering Sea. The end of the Rockies. The final American wilderness.

Where is he?

The willow leaves flash their silvery undersides in the wind, McCone poppies and the purple lupine and red bayrose and yellow composites dance on the hillsides. Wordsworth would enjoy the spectacle. I think. But he might not care much for what I'm waiting for. Expecting. Both shotguns lean on the last pile of duffle where John lies sleeping, out of sight, out of hearing. I am unarmed, ready, open. Let it come.

Two shrikes watch me from the willows. Three screaming gulls pursue a golden eagle high above the river, diving and pecking at its head, trying to turn it into a bald eagle. I long to see that eagle flip on its back in midair, snatch one of those gulls in its deadly talons and—*rip its head off!* But the eagle sails on in straight, steady airline toward the hills, and the gulls drop away, bored.

My bear does not come.

As the plane takes off Gil says, "I'm going to show you something." He banks and turns off course and enters a pass through the foothills west of the river. We fly a thousand feet above the lion-colored tundra. Little ponds and bogholes wink, sparkle, glitter in the light. We cross another ridge.

And there below, suddenly, the hills appear to be in motion, alive, as if the skin of the earth had begun to crawl over its rock-bound bones. A broad river of caribou streams in waves west-southwesterly up the ridges and through the valleys, all its elements in rapid, parallel advance. It takes me a moment to realize that I am looking down on the greatest mass movement of un-tamed four-hooved animals I may ever see. It's like the stampede of the wildebeests on the Serengeti Plain.

"My God," I say. "How many?"

Gil banks and circles, looking down. "Hard to tell. It's only a part of the Porcupine River herd. Maybe forty, maybe fifty thousand."

John and Maureen are busy taking pictures. I'm too excited to get out my binoculars. "Any GRIZZ down there?"

Gil looks again. "Bound to be a few," he says. "But they blend in so well we'd never see them."

He circles one more time, giving us all a good look, then bears northwest for Barter Island and Kaktovik, over the last foothills and two thousand feet above the coastal plain. Well, I'm thinking, now I'm satisfied. Now I've seen it, the secret of the essence of the riddle of the Spirit of the Arctic—the flowering of life, of life wild, free and abundant, in the midst of the hardest, cruelest land on the northern half of Earth.

And then, as we approach the coast and the tiny island at its edge, the frozen sea appears again, the ocean of ice, the crescent rim of *whiteness* stretching on, and on, and on, unbroken, apparently unlimited, toward the hazy stillness of the polar climax— and beyond. What can I say of that? The vision chills both thought and emotion.

What can I say except confess that I have seen but little of the real North, and of that little understood less. The planet is bigger than we ever imagined. The world is colder, more ancient, more strange and more mysterious than we had dreamed. And we puny human creatures with our many tools and toys and fears and hopes make only one small leaf on the great efflorescing tree of life.

Too much. No equation however organic, no prose however royally purple, can bracket our world within the boundaries of mind.

So what. "Gil," I say. "Doctor Gil Zemansky."

"Yes?" he says.

"Buy us a beer in downtown Kaktovik."

"I'll buy two," says Gil. "One for you and one for me."